C H A P T E R   I

KU-778-315

SOCIETY AND
POLITICAL CULTURE

NATION AND NATIONALITY

A nation is defined as a people sharing a common history, language, culture, set of beliefs, race and way of life. In most cases, a nation also occupies one geographical locale. Its national identity or nationality are those characteristics of its past, its culture and its way of life that provide a feeling of belonging. Flags, anthems, pledges, national holidays, and sport all contribute to a person's sense of belonging to a nation.

The symbols and emblems of nationality can be very powerful and persuasive. They create a strong bond between people, and between people and their country. How else can we explain why, over the centuries, people have willingly fought and died to defend their nation's interests?

In the nineteenth century, people believed that each nation should have its own political system known as the **nation-state.** This belief is called **nationalism**.

Some states were formed by uniting more than one nation. The United Kingdom, for example, consists of members of the English, Welsh, Scottish and Irish nations. Other states became colonies of larger ones.

Nationalism is also linked to the struggle for independence and self-determination. Throughout the twentieth century, many nations of Africa and Asia have won their independence and formed self-governing states. The Irish state was established in this way in 1922.

nation-state:
the political entity of the nation – people who share a common history, language, territory, culture and beliefs

nationalism:
the belief in or devotion to the aspirations of one's nation

IRELAND IN TRANSITION

monolithic:
made of only one or to be all the same

Ireland is a **monolithic** society. This means that the overwhelming majority of Irish people share the same characteristics; 97 per cent of them are white Roman Catholics who, like their parents, were born in Ireland of Irish parents. They speak English despite the constitution's claim that Irish is the official language. Today only 2 per cent of the population can speak Irish fluently.

Ireland has few ethnic or religious minorities because it has been unaffected by waves of migration from Asia, Africa or the Middle East. Since 1841, there has been a continual decline in population due to famine and emigration. Today only 3.5m people live in the Republic of Ireland compared to 6.5m living in the same area in 1841.

Ireland is also a society in transition. In the 1950s, Irish society was primarily rural with almost 40 per cent of its labour force working in agriculture. Educational and employment opportunities were limited; jobs in banking, school teaching, nursing and religious life were highly desired. Those unable to find work in Ireland emigrated – usually to Britain but often to the United States.

The vast majority of the population, however, lived most of their lives in the same neighbourhood among people who shared the same religious beliefs, and the same moral and cultural values. People learned about the world by listening to Radio Éireann or reading Irish newspapers. Travel was limited to the wealthy few while books and films were subjected to strict censorship. Members of a family usually voted for the same political party, depending on which side that family fought during the civil war. Ireland was a conservative, stable island society based around tight-knit communities and family life.

Éamon de Valera highlighted what he saw as the benefits of this way of life:

The Ireland which we dreamed of would be the home of a people who valued material wealth only as a basis of right living, of a people who were satisfied with frugal comfort and devoted their leisure to things of the spirit; a land whose countryside would be bright with cosy homesteads, whose fields and villages would be joyous with the sounds of industry, with the rompings of sturdy children, the contests of athletic youths and the laughter of happy maidens, whose firesides would be forums for the wisdom of serene old age. It would, in a word, be the home of a people living the life that God desires that man should live.

St Patrick's Day, 1944

Today, much of this has changed. 1958 is considered to be the milestone in the evolution of Irish society from a rural agricultural society to an urban industrial society, participating in the world economy. The swiftness of this change sets Ireland apart from most other European countries which experienced similar changes but over a much longer period of time.

More Irish people now live in towns and cities. One-third of the population lives in Dublin and its surrounding communities, while only four out of every ten people live in rural areas. They favour individualised lifestyles in marriage and family life. Their religious and moral beliefs are more likely to be a private affair. Young people are less influenced by how their parents vote, choosing candidates according to a wider range of issues and values.

Closer contact with the rest of Europe, due to our membership of the European Union, has had a major impact on many aspects of Irish life. Continental holidays are not unusual. Where once we could only see RTE, British stations, cable and satellite dishes now bring us any number of programmes from across Europe. Our shops are full of products which have been imported from all over the continent. The range of food served by restaurants compares well with that of any developed society.

The success of rock bands such as U2, of authors such as Roddy Doyle, and of Irish film-making has promoted Ireland as a cultural and literary focal point. Success in international sport has raised our status in the eyes of other countries and boosted national pride. Irish people no longer see themselves living on an island, but as part of Europe.

RODDY DOYLE
Paddy Clarke Ha Ha Ha

ASSIGNMENTS

1 Give some examples of the use of symbols or emblems that signify Irishness.
2 What events or individuals have given you a pride in being Irish?
3 What do people mean by the term traditional values ?
4 What are the characteristics of Irish culture today?

ACTIVITIES

1 Films and television programmes portray Irish people in various ways.
   Look at one of the following films:
   The Quiet Man (dir. John Ford)
   Darby O'Gill and the Little People (dir. Robert Stevenson)
   The Field (dir. Jim Sheridan)
   The Commitments (dir. Alan Parker)
   Patriot Games (dir. Philip Noyce).
   (a) What view of Irish society is portrayed in the film?
   (b) Do you think it presents a fair or true representation of Irish people?
   (c) Do you find any aspect of the film's image of Ireland or of Irish people offensive?
2 Organise a classroom discussion around the photographs on the following pages.
   Consider each of the following:
   (a) Describe what is happening in each photograph.
   (b) Where do you think these photographs might be used: in IDA or Bord Fáilte publicity material? in national or international newspapers? Why might different groups choose to emphasise different characteristics?
   (c) Write a caption for each photograph.
   (d) What message do you think each of the photographs conveys?
   (e) What image of Ireland do you think a person from another country might have having looked at these photographs?

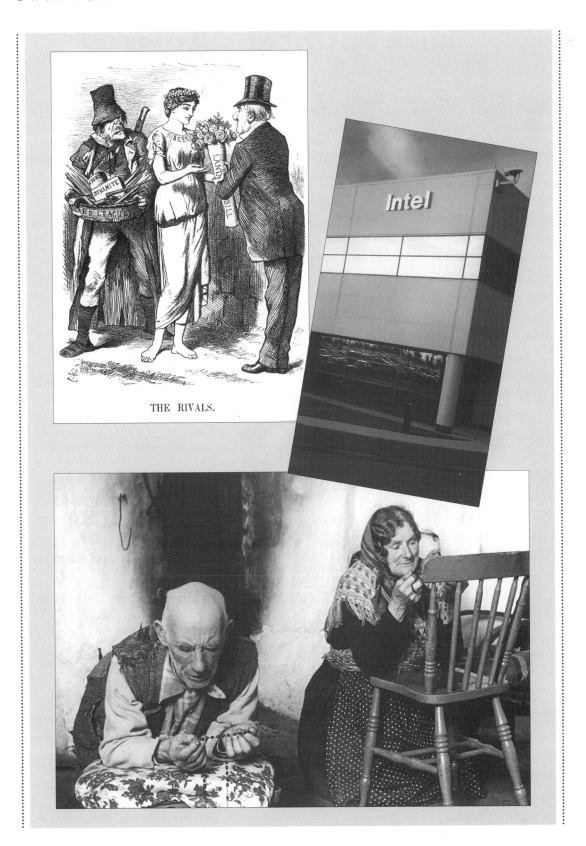

THE RIVALS.

IRISH POLITICAL CULTURE

The basic values, beliefs and expectations of a society constitute its political culture. A society's **political culture** is strongly influenced by how that society came into existence, by the people's trust in how decisions are made and by their general level of satisfaction. As a society develops, its political values might also change. Beliefs and attitudes that were once important may no longer be so important. New attitudes may develop along with social and economic change.

Ireland has recently undergone a dramatic and rapid transformation. In what ways has Irish society changed? What developments and ideas have been most influential in this process of change? Has this change affected how people define their 'Irishness'? Has it affected political and cultural values?

The main influences on the formation and development of Irish history, society, political institutions and culture have been the following:

*   the colonial experience
*   Gaelic culture, language and tradition
*   the legacy of British rule
*   Irish Catholicism.

THE COLONIAL EXPERIENCE

Ireland is an island on the edge of the British Isles, at the periphery of the European continent. The geographical closeness of Ireland and Britain made the smaller island an attractive target for invasion and conquest. Eight hundred years ago it became an English colony with its economic, social and political life dominated by London.

Religion was the main distinction between the settlers and the Gaels. Each group had their own culture and customs. These differences laid the foundation for the emergence of two distinct communities on the island. People desiring full independence for Ireland became known as nationalists. Those wanting Ireland to remain part of the United Kingdom were known as unionists.

In 1922, the island was partitioned because there was no consensus or common view about the future status of Ireland. Northern Ireland remained part of the United Kingdom; the Republic of Ireland, called Éire in the constitution, became an independent state.

The influence of the Irish state does not extend over the entire island or include everyone who calls himself or herself Irish, or whom some may consider to be Irish. Many people living in Northern Ireland, for example, prefer to consider themselves British or Ulster men and women.

Failure to win independence for the entire island left many people feeling that

political culture:
what people think about politics – their beliefs, values and aspirations

8

the national revolution was incomplete. The desire to win full independence or to unite the island into a 32-county Irish republic has persisted.

In recent years, there has been a growing recognition among people living in the Republic and in Northern Ireland that unity may not be possible. Many people realise that the two societies have developed differently and apart.

A SOLDIER'S SONG

1
We'll sing a song, a soldier's song,
With cheering rousing chorus,
As round our blazing fires we throng,
The starry heavens o'er us;
Impatient for the coming fight,
And as we 'wait the morning's light,
Here in the silence of the night,
We'll chant a soldier's song.

CHORUS
Soldiers are we, whose lives are pledged to Ireland;
Some have come from a land beyond the wave.
Sworn to be free, no more our ancient sire-land
Shall shelter the despot or the slave.
Tonight we man the 'bearna baol',
In Erin's cause come woe or weal;
Mid cannon's roar and rifle's peal
We'll chant a soldier's song.

2
In valley green or towering crag
Our fathers fought before us,
And conquered 'neath the same old flag
That's proudly floating o'er us,
We're children of a fighting race
That never yet has known disgrace,
And as we march to face the foe,
We'll chant a soldier's song.

CHORUS
3
Song of the Gael! Men of the Pale!
The long watched day is breaking;
The serried ranks of Innisfail
Shall set the tyrant quaking.
Our camp fires now are burning low;
See in the east a silv'ry glow,
Our young 'waits the Saxon foe,
So chant a soldier's song.

CHORUS

Written by Peadar Kearney

THE ISLAND

They say the skies of Lebanon are burning
Those mighty cedars bleeding in the heat
They're showing pictures on the television
Women and children dying in the street
And we're still at it in our own place
Still trying to reach the future thru' the past
Still trying to carve tomorrow from a tombstone.

But hey! Don't listen to me!
'Cos this wasn't meant to be no sad song
We've heard too much of that before
Right now I only want to be here with you
Till the morning dew comes falling
I want to take you to the island
And trace your footprints in the sand
And in the evening when the sun goes down
We'll make love to the sound of the ocean.

They're raising banners over by the markets
Whitewashing slogans on the shipyard walls
Witch doctors praying for a mighty showdown
No way our holy flag is gonna fall
Up here we sacrifice our children
To feed the worn-out dreams of yesterday
And teach them dying will lead us into glory.

But hey! Don't listen ...

Now I know us plain folks don't see all the story
And I know this peace and love's just copping out
And I guess these young boys dying in the ditches
Is just what being free is all about
And how this twisted wreckage down on Main Street
Will bring us all together in the end
And we'll go marching down the road to freedom
Freedom.

Written by Paul Brady

ASSIGNMENT

The words of *A Soldier's Song* and *The Island* suggest a difference in how people define their 'Irishness'. Compare the songs and answer these questions.

(a) What is each song about?

(b) What message does each convey?

(c) What does Paul Brady mean in the following lines?

     Up here we sacrifice our children

     To feed the worn-out dreams of yesterday

     And teach them dying will lead us into glory.

(d) What was the historical background to *A Soldier's Song*?

(e) How do the songs differ?

GAELIC CULTURE, LANGUAGE AND TRADITION

Each nation has a distinctive cultural tradition. This tradition is influenced by how the society has developed and how its people live. Irish culture and society have been strongly influenced by several invasions.

James Connolly, the Irish socialist, believed that prior to the invasions, Celtic Ireland had been a peaceful, sophisticated society with its own Brehon laws.

Here then is the conquest. Fix it clearly before your eyes. National liberty, personal liberty, social security all gone, the country ruled from its highest down to its meanest office by foreigners; the Irish race landless, homeless, living by sufferance upon the mercy of their masters ...

     The Reconquest of Ireland, 1915

Over the centuries, the British way of life became more and more influential.

The revival of Gaelic culture began in the nineteenth century. Irish literature, song, poetry, drama and sport combined to create a powerful Gaelic-Irish identity. The Gaelic Athletic Association or GAA (1884) promoted Gaelic football and hurling, excluding members of the Crown forces or those playing foreign sports such as rugby or soccer. The Gaelic League (1893) and the National Literary Society (1892) were formed to restore or promote the Irish language and all literary aspects of Irish culture.

Authors such as James Joyce and J. M. Synge, whose writings presented an unflattering picture of Ireland, were harassed. Joyce felt compelled to leave the country while one of Synge's plays, *The Playboy of the Western World*, caused riots when it was performed in 1907 at the Abbey Theatre.

Rome rule:

the suggestion that Roman Catholic religious values dominate law and society

In the decades following independence, speaking Irish, learning Irish dancing or playing Gaelic games became powerful symbols of Irishness. Foreign films and literature were discouraged. Irishness became closely identified with the majority religion. Unionists referred to this as **Rome rule**.

Given Ireland's history, different traditions and loyalties, it is not surprising that Irish culture has often caused division among people. Many Northern Ireland nationalists regard speaking Irish, displaying the tricolour, and having Irish street signs as an expression of their Irishness. On the other hand many of their neighbours identify with Ulster, Northern Ireland or the United Kingdom, and display the Union Jack outside their homes.

ASSIGNMENTS

1 Look up the names of other writers involved in the Irish literary revival.
2 Which Dublin theatre was founded to renew interest in Irish drama?
3 What kinds of foreign influences were criticised by supporters of the Celtic revival?
4 Do you think it is possible for people to be both British and Irish? Why do some people object to this?

ACTIVITIES

1 Read either some of the stories of James Joyce's *Dubliners* or J. M. Synge's *The Playboy of the Western World*.
   (a) What picture of Ireland emerges from these stories?
   (b) Why do you think Synge's play provoked such strong reaction from people in Ireland at the time?
2 Organise a classroom debate: That GAA pitches should be used by soccer teams.

THE LEGACY OF BRITISH RULE

The Irish Free State inherited a strong tradition of parliamentary democracy from the British. Under the Act of Union, Irish politicians like Daniel O'Connell (1745-1833) and Charles Stewart Parnell (1846-1891) were elected to the House of Commons. There they learned about political debate, parliamentary procedure and lawmaking.

By 1900, new local government structures and electoral laws allowed ordinary people in Ireland to run for election and hold public office. Laws providing for welfare, pensions and public health put Irish people on a par with other British citizens. An extensive primary education system, rail and road communications, and a public administration system were well established by the early 1900s. These developments made the transition to independence relatively peaceful.

In spite of being revolutionaries, the founding fathers copied the **Westminster model** for Irish parliamentary procedures and government structures, and the **Whitehall model** for the civil service.

Custom House, Dublin

The Garda Síochána was established in 1924 as an unarmed police force similar to the British system. All the major institutions of the state, from the post office to the legal system, have been strongly influenced by Britain. Many judicial decisions are based on British legal precedent, and some Irish law predates the founding of the state.

After years of being ruled from London, it is hardly surprising that anti-Britishness has formed an important part of the Irish identity. It was one of the reasons why Éamon de Valera proposed a new constitution in 1937 and why the Irish government pursued a policy of neutrality during World War II. It did not want to be

Westminster model: *system of government based on the UK's, its name comes from the fact that the British Parliament is located in the area of London called Westminster*

Whitehall model: *system of central administration based on the British civil service, its name comes from the fact that its headquarter is located in the area of London called Whitehall.*

Éamon de Valera and Fianna Fáil party leaders leaving Leinster House having refused to take the Oath of Allegiance, 1927.

seen to be supporting Britain in any international situation. De Valera went out of his way to prove Ireland's neutrality when he visited the German embassy to express condolences on the death of Adolf Hitler.

It has always been very curious to me how Irish sentiment sticks in this half-way house – how it continues to apparently hate the English, and at the same time continues to imitate them; how it continues to clamour for recognition as a distinct nationality, and at the same time throws away with both hands what would make it so.

Douglas Hyde, The Necessity for de-Anglicising Ireland, 1892

Despite these expressions of anti-British sentiment, relations between the two islands is very close. Irish citizens travel freely to and from Britain with no passport demands, are entitled to claim social welfare and housing benefit there, and can vote in British general elections. Over 60 per cent of Irish households view British and Northern Ireland television programmes, listen to British radio, and read British newspapers and magazines. Many Irish people have emigrated to Britain; today, lots of Irish people have some family member(s) living there.

ASSIGNMENTS

1   Many of our major public buildings were built during the time of the British administration in Ireland. Name three of them.
2   What aspects of Irish life have been strongly influenced by Britain?
3   Which other European countries remained neutral during World War II?
4   Do Irish people express any anti-Britishness today?

RESEARCH ACTIVITY

Why do you think Douglas Hyde was chosen as the first President of Ireland in 1938?

ACTIVITIES

1   Which newspapers sold in Ireland today are Irish-owned? Which ones are British-owned? Try to find out how many copies of each one are sold each day. Which ones are most popular? Why do you think some are more popular than others?
2   Write a diary listing all the television programmes watched by members of your household during the week.
    (a) How many of them are Irish-made programmes?
    (b) How many are British-made?
    (c) Why do you think people choose to watch the programmes they do?
    (d) Which television channels are preferred? Why?

IRISH CATHOLICISM

Catholicism has enjoyed a particularly strong and influential relationship with the Irish people. Unlike its counterparts on the continent, the Irish church was neither the established church nor an owner of great wealth or landholdings. The state never made episcopal appointments. Instead, the church became strongly associated with the tenant-farmer and Irish nationalism.

By the end of the nineteenth century the church had developed an extensive network of hospitals, social services, and primary schools. In this way it played an important role in modernising Irish society and educating the population. After independence it continued to provide basic educational and health services without which the new state could not have survived.

This closeness stems from the fact that the population and its politicians are overwhelmingly of the same religion. Also, Ireland has a particularly large majority of committed and practising Catholics. In 1990, 85 per cent of the population attended mass at least weekly compared to only 42 per cent for Europe as a whole. Irish people are more likely to believe in Hell, the Devil, Heaven, God, life after death, and sin than are their European neighbours.

The European Values Survey 1990, shows that there are variations in the level

MORE LIKELY TO ATTEND MASS	LESS LIKELY TO ATTEND MASS
• women	• men
• women working in the home	• women working outside the home
• older people	• young people (born since 1950s)
• less educated	• people with third-level education
• rural dwellers	• urban dwellers
• employed	• unemployed

from C. Whelan (ed), *Values and Social Change in Ireland*, 1994

of religious attendance in Ireland.

Irish people differ on whether the church has the right answers for today's problems. While many feel the church should speak out on social issues, others question its right to criticise government policy or discuss personal morality. Many Irish Catholics are choosing their own solutions to individual problems. Some believe that, in order to encourage closer links with Northern Ireland, there must be greater separation of church and state.

Does this mean that Irish society is becoming **secularised**? The removal of the special position of the church from the constitution in 1972 was a step in this direction. The sharp decline in young people following a religious vocation has reduced the number of teaching and nursing religious. This will have a gradual effect on the church's influence in education and social services. Since mass attendance is influenced by whether someone lives in an urban area and was born after 1950, there is likely to be a decline in attendances in the future.

Religion, however, remains a powerful influence on Irish society. The constitution and some legislation retains a strong commitment to Catholic social and moral values. Rather than rejecting religion, many Irish people are redefining their attitude towards it.

secularised:

the separation of religious beliefs from the affairs of society and state

ACTIVITIES

1 Organise a classroom discussion on personal and civic morality. Using the permissiveness scale from the European Values Survey 1990, make 1 = never justified and 10 = always justified. Consider each of the following issues and score everyone's view. Then make a chart indicating everyone's answers. What kind of pattern emerges? What does it tell us about Irish society today?

PERSONAL MORALITY
- adultery
- sexual relations under the legal age of consent
- homosexuality
- prostitution
- abortion
- divorce
- euthanasia
- suicide

CIVIC MORALITY
- claiming state benefits illegally
- avoiding a fare on public transport
- buying something knowing that it was stolen
- taking a car that is not one's own
- taking marijuana or hashish
- keeping money that one has found
- cheating or lying in one's own interest
- accepting a bribe in the course of one's duties
- failing to report damage done accidentally to a vehicle
- threatening workers who refuse to join a strike
- killing in self-defence

2   Organise a classroom debate: That it is proper for the church to speak out on issues of personal morality; on issues of third-world problems; on issues of unemployment.

3   Are there any members of religious or ethnic minorities living in your community? Invite some representatives to visit your class and discuss with them their religious or cultural beliefs. In what way do their beliefs differ from your own? How do they feel about being a member of a minority community?

A CHANGING SOCIETY?

INDUSTRIALISATION AND URBANISATION

The industrial revolution came late to Ireland. Until the late 1950s, Ireland could still be described as an agricultural society. Only the north-east of the island, around Belfast, experienced any sizeable industrial growth. During the nineteenth century, the linen industry, shipbuilding, and engineering were the largest employers.

Economic development was much slower in the south. Agriculture, cattle or sheep, and crop-growing (tillage) were the primary enterprises. Even though Ireland had one of the most extensive rail and road networks at the time, there was little work available in the towns or cities. Many people emigrated, usually to Britain, in search of work.

At the time of independence, little had changed. Ireland was still overly-dependent on agriculture. Limited growth occurred in the 1930s. New policies were needed to develop the economy and provide jobs. Sean Lemass's *Programme for Economic Expansion* in 1958 is credited with bringing about an industrial revolution in Ireland.

Traditional manufacturing industries were replaced in the 1970s by jobs in commerce, insurance, finance and public administration. There were also new opportunities in high-technology jobs in the electronic, telecommunication, chemical and pharmaceutical areas. Many new employers were American, German and Japanese multi-nationals. Living standards improved and the rate of emigration slowed for a short time.

Urbanisation occurred side-by-side with the expansion of industry. People left rural Ireland in search of work in new factories located in the towns and cities. The movement of people out of agriculture has been so great that people speak of the decline of the west.

Irish society was gradually transformed. By 1981, the bulk of the population was living in urban centres around the country. As a result of Dublin's dominant position, there is a concentration of government and public offices, media, financial headquarters and educational institutions in the east.

urbanisation: *the process by which more and more people live in cities*

AMERICAN VISITOR: "I suppose you rear these calves for export?"
FARMER: "Yes, indeed, Sir. Same as the children!"

Dublin Opinion, Sept. 1924.

EMPLOYMENT, UNEMPLOYMENT AND EMIGRATION

Unemployment is common to all societies. The level of unemployment, however, varies. Ireland has a history of high unemployment despite its small population. Today (1995), c. 17 per cent of the population are officially registered as unemployed. This figure would be much higher if everyone currently on a community or social employment scheme were included. There are fewer people at work today than in the 1930s.

The main reason for high unemployment is the lack of jobs. In order to provide employment for everyone who is currently unemployed and for school-leavers, 30,000 new jobs need to be created each year. This is a difficult, though not impossible, task. Political parties regularly discuss which policies to implement in order to create employment. Their choice of policy is a political decision.

During the nineteenth century some economists claimed that poverty and famine in Ireland were due to too many people, or overpopulation. To help improve the living standards of the population as a whole, over 40,000 people were encouraged to emigrate to the USA, Canada, Australia and New Zealand. Emigration has often been seen as the only solution to unemployment.

Irish emigrants have gone wherever employment opportunities were best. Most emigrants were unskilled males from rural areas who sought work in industry, on the railroads or in construction. Women also left. As females, they could not inherit the family farm and were forced to find work as domestic servants, nurses or office workers.

Today, Irish emigrants are likely to be highly educated and come from urban areas. Approximately 25 per cent of third-level graduates are now living abroad. Continuing high unemployment in Ireland will probably mean that emigration will continue into the next century. This makes Ireland a labour-exporting economy.

What we have now is a very literate emigrant who thinks nothing of coming to the United States and going back to Ireland and maybe on to Germany and back to Ireland again ... The world is now one world and they can always return to Ireland with the skills they have developed. We regard them as part of a global generation of Irish people. We shouldn't be defeatist or pessimistic about it. We should be proud of it. After all, we can't all live on a small island.

Brian Lenihan, TD (FF), former Tánaiste and Minister for Foreign Affairs, 1987

SOCIAL STRUCTURE

Within Irish society today, there are perhaps ... smaller Irelands ... Rural Ireland and Urban Ireland, ... the respective territories of what in the simple good old days were known as Culchie and Jackeen. When I was growing up, this was the great rivalry. Dublin was identified with people with hard, Joxer accents who made fun of people from the country. The two sides met on rare occasions, like the All-Ireland Final, when they would throw harmless abuse at each other outside Croke Park, occasionally resorting to fisticuffs ...

It was not long before it occurred to me that there were at least two Dublins ... geographically divided by the river Liffey. When you crossed O'Connell Bridge from the southside, you became aware within a few yards that you were among different people than you had been encountering just a couple of streets before. Something about their appearance and dress set them apart. The men wore leather jackets, windcheaters, jumpers, T-shirts, sneakers and white socks. The women all seemed to have their hair dyed blonde. They spoke with rough, Joxer accents ...

Less than a mile away, on the southside ... [was] Grafton Street, Baggot Street and Merrion Row ... This was official Dublin, a thriving metropolis inhabited by well-heeled and fashionable people who, as they themselves would have it, worked hard and played hard. This Dublin was the centre of the nation's economy, government and media. The other Dublin was the place we had seen from time to time ... [on television] – a Dublin of poverty, neglect, alienation, drug addiction and very little hope of real change ... When the two Dublins came into contact, it was either by accident or for the purposes of the war that was being waged between them – a war called crime.

John Waters, *Jiving at the Crossroads*, 1991

The Irish constitution states that everyone is treated equally before the law. Every citizen has one vote. This is known as political equality. It is not the same as economic equality.

Everyone in Ireland, as in every society, does not have the same income, wealth, experiences or status in society. These inequalities divide people into different groups called **social strata** or social classes. The social structure presents an over-view of how a society is organised. The social structure looks like layers of sedimentary rock. Each layer is equal to a social class or strata in society. People within each class share similar life chances or opportunities, and attitudes. Movement up or down in the social structure is called social mobility.

According to Combat Poverty (1988), up to one third of the Irish population could be described as living in poverty. They are members of a growing class in society who are trapped in a cycle of unemployment or low paid work, poor housing, low educational achievement and poor health. Many are dependent on social welfare to survive.

social strata:

a term used to describe the organisation of society into different groups or classes of people who share certain characteristics of income, lifestyle and opportunities

The social structure is often pictured as a triangle. The most powerful in society are the least numerous and stand at the top.

One way of showing the huge gap between the wealthiest and the poorest in society is by examining who really owns the wealth of the country. Approximately 5 per cent of the population owns about 60–63 per cent of all personal wealth (bank deposits, share holdings, houses). These are 1975 figures. They are possibly exaggerated but they show that, at that time, Ireland was highly unequal. Today, more people own their home and have bank accounts, but the inequalities remain.

A study by Micheal McGreil S.J., *Prejudice and Tolerance in Ireland* (1973), shows that Dublin is a segregated city. People of different social classes live separate lives and may never meet.

Is it possible for the son or daughter of an unskilled person to become a doctor? Children of middle-class parents enjoy a substantial advantage over children whose parents are unskilled or unemployed. Forty-two per cent of unskilled people are likely to be deprived compared to only 0.7 per cent of higher professionals (ESRI, 1990).

WHO GOES TO COLLEGE?

The further west you are born or the more advantaged you are, the more likely you are to sit the Leaving Cert and the higher your chances of going to college.

- 86 per cent of young people in the west sit the Leaving Cert, 82 per cent in the south-east, but only 76 per cent in Dublin and 70 per cent in the east.
- 80 per cent of Mayo young people entered college in 1993 compared to only 48 per cent of Dublin young people.
- 67 per cent of young people from the Dublin 6 area went on to higher education but only 8 per cent from Ballyfermot.
- Children of farmers are more likely to go to college than the children of skilled or unskilled manual workers.

from the *Steering Committee on the Future Development of Higher Education*, 1994.

Gender (being male or female), race, age and religion also heavily influence people's life chances. Opportunities for women are expanding but are still very limited. If they are employed outside the home, it is usually in low-paid, part-time jobs with little promotional opportunity.

People often face hidden discrimination because of their race or religion. Catholics in Northern Ireland were denied access to certain jobs for many years.

All these factors limit the opportunity for people to participate fully in society.

They also inhibit people's ability to move up in the social structure.

The following is one way to describe the Irish social structure of today:

- large proprietors (agricultural and non-agricultural employers; property owners)
- small proprietors (small employers, property owners)
- middle-class (professional and other non-manual workers)
- working class (manual and service workers)
- unemployed.

A NEW IDENTITY?

In recent years, Ireland has become more and more similar to other developed societies. This change can be viewed as either good or bad, beneficial or detrimental – depending on your point of view.

For some people, the transformation of Ireland from an isolated conservative backwater of Europe to an outward-looking society sharing similar values and lifestyles with the richer and more developed European countries has been welcome. Some people are less happy, believing that the process of modernisation has led to the devaluation of our unique and traditional lifestyle, and a decline in moral and social values. Others believe that in trying to become more like other developed societies, Ireland is losing what makes it unique.

Economic development and membership of the European Union have been significant factors in Ireland's transformation from a rural agricultural to an urban industrial society. Ireland is ranked the 23rd wealthiest country in the world according to the World Bank. Despite continued high unemployment, Irish people today enjoy a better lifestyle and more opportunities than their parents did. They see their futures and their children's futures as part of Europe.

In recent years, a new Irish culture can be seen emerging – one that is heavily influenced by tradition but is open to new and different experiences. Traditional musicians play side-by-side with blues, rock and country musicians while Irish dancing uses techniques of modern dance and ballet. The Irish language is no longer confined to people living in the west of Ireland. Clannad, Enya and Hot House Flowers have had huge success, in Ireland and abroad, with songs in Irish. Irish sports fans have no difficulty supporting British soccer.

As urbanisation draws more and more people away from small villages and towns, rural Ireland is in decline. Lack of jobs also forces young people to move away. The population of many western counties is falling. Fewer people require fewer services; post offices and garda stations are closing. Picturesque cottages are being bought up by foreigners as holiday homes.

Lifestyles are also changing. With greater opportunities available, many young people are choosing to marry late or not at all. Sexual practices are also changing. Few people still leave their keys in the latch. Drugs, poverty and long-term unemployment have contributed to rising crime. Some people blame this on the lack of parental control and a collapse of moral values.

Both viewpoints see change simply as good or bad, positive or negative. The process of change and the consequences are, however, much more complicated. There is no single path to becoming a modern society just as there is no single way of growing up. Individuals carve out unique and diverse experiences – so do nations. The richness of a nation's history and culture means that its path of development can never be the same as its neighbour's.

ASSIGNMENTS

1 What kind of society was Ireland before the 1960s?

2 Who is credited with helping to make Ireland a modern industrial economy?

3 When people talk of the decline of the west what do you think they mean?

4 Why has emigration often been described as the traditional solution to unemployment ?

5 What were the factors that forced some Irish women into emigration?

6 What do you think are the main differences between the emigrants of the 1950s and emigrants of today?

7 How would you classify people as either poor or well off ? List ten criteria.

8 What is meant by the term 'the poverty trap'?

9 What does the term social mobility mean?

10 Do you think it is easier for the son or daughter of a doctor to become a doctor than for the son or daughter of an unskilled worker? List your reasons.

11 In what way can gender (being male or female), race, age or religion influence people's life chances?

12 Look again at the description of the Irish social structure outlined on page 20.

    (a) Do you agree that Irish society is divided into these different social strata or classes?

    (b) Can you describe the type of people who might fit into each of these strata or classes?

    (c) Are the 'unemployed' a separate social class?

RESEARCH ACTIVITIES

1 Make a collage using postcards, photographs, magazines or newspapers to reflect your view of Ireland today.

2 Find or describe a photograph or image of Ireland which you find offensive. Why do you find it so?

ACTIVITIES

1 Organise a classroom discussion: What are the causes of unemployment in Ireland? Which policies would you choose to implement in order to end unemployment?

2 Organise a classroom debate: That Ireland is becoming a two-tier society.

3 Do you think the transformation of Ireland from an isolated conservative backwater of Europe to an outward-looking society sharing similar values and lifestyles with the richer and more developed European countries is a welcome or unwelcome development?

President DeValera and his Cabinet

Seán Mac an tSaoi
Aire Airgid
Seán MacEntee, TD
Minister for Finance

Seán Leimeas,
Aire Tionnscail 7 Tráchtála
Seán F. Lemass, T.D.
Minister for Industry
and Commerce

Seosaiṁ Ó Conġaile
Aire Tailte 7 Iascaig
Senator Joseph Connolly,
Minister for Lands and Fisheries

Séamus Ó Riain,
Aire Talṁaíoċta
James Ryan, M.B.,T.D.
Minister for Agriculture

Éamonn de Valéra, B.A., B.Sc., LL.D.
Uaċtarán 7 Aire Gnóta Coigríce
President and Minister for External Affairs

Proinnsias Ó hAodaġáin
Aire Cosanta
Frank Aiken, T.D.
Minister for Defence

S.T. Ó Ceallaiġ
Leas-Uaċtarán agus
Aire Rialtais Áitiúla
agus Sláinte Puiblí
Seán T. O'Kelly, T.D.
Vice President
and Minister for
Local Government
and
Public Health

Tomás Ó Deirg
Aire Oideaċais
Thomas Derrig, T.D.
Minister for Education

Seanóid Ó Beólán
Aire Puist 7 Telegrapa
Gerald Boland, T.D.
Minister for Posts and
Telegraphs

Pádraig Ruitléis
Aire Dlí 7 Cirt
Patrick J. Ruttledge, T.D.
Minister for Justice

POLITICS AND GOVERNMENT

WHAT IS SOCIETY?

There are always likely to be differing opinions and interests among a group of people. A family may disagree over who should do certain chores such as the cooking or washing up. Friends might argue about which film to go and see. You may come into conflict with your parents about the type of clothes you want to wear or the kind of music you like to hear. You could also come into conflict with your teachers concerning class discipline and project deadlines.

On a larger scale, groups of people will have different opinions about how society should be organised. It is difficult to get people to agree on a single course of action, to agree what policies are to be implemented or how natural resources (land, water, fish, oil/gas and forests) should be owned, controlled and distributed. Differences of opinion are resolved through custom, discussion, bargaining, voting or occasionally through violence.

Large numbers of people living together in an organised community are known as a society. Societies develop a set of rules, regulations and principles to help them make decisions that affect the community. The bigger and more complicated a society is, the more it needs to develop a system of government. Just as a family needs to decide who will do the household chores, society needs a structure so that its members can live in harmony.

The following is a list of different groups of people in order of size and complexity, beginning with the smallest unit:

- Family
- Friends
- Social or Sports Club
- School or College
- Neighbourhood or Townland
- Village, Town, City
- Country
- European Union
- International organisations.

ASSIGNMENT

The larger and more diverse a group of people are, the more complex the rules must be to ensure harmony and fairness. Look at the list of different groups of people on page 24.

(a) How does each of these groups attempt to maintain harmony?

(b) List some conflicts that have occurred among members of any of these groups.

(c) Outline some of the rules you have experienced in any of these groups.

ACTIVITIES

1 Your school is a social organisation.

   (a) How is your school organised?

   (b) Does your school have rules? Name some of them. Which ones do you agree with? Which ones do you disagree with?

   (c) Does your school have a students' council? What role does the council play?

   (d) Do you think the students' council has sufficient influence in the school?

   (e) Organise a role-play of a meeting between students, teachers, the board of management and parents in which you discuss plans to organise a disco in the school.

2 You and your friends are planning to go on a camping trip together.

   (a) Devise a list of rules to ensure harmony and safety.

   (b) Outline the different areas of responsibilities. You might consider: should there be a kitty? who will control it? who will do the shopping? who will do the cooking and cleaning?

   (c) List some of the conflicts that you may encounter on the trip.

3 There are a number of ways for a family to organise the washing up.
Give a solution to this problem choosing from the following criteria: by custom, by discussion, by bargaining, or by violence.

4 You have a late-night party in your house. Act out or list some of the disagreements that you, your family or your friends may encounter when dealing with neighbours. Give a brief synopsis of your side of the events and then give your neighbours' point of view.

WHAT IS GOVERNMENT?

Living in a society is not only about structures and rules. Societies also seek to establish principles by which to govern themselves. In most democracies, these principles are based around ideas of freedom, equality and justice. Politics is the means by which we achieve these principles or goals.

In the future days, which we seek to make secure, we look forward to a world founded upon four essential freedoms. The first is freedom of speech and expression everywhere in the world. The second is freedom of every person to worship God in his own way everywhere in the world. The third is freedom from want everywhere in the world. The fourth is freedom from fear everywhere in the world.

Franklin Delano Roosevelt,
President, USA, 1941

Governments are created to bring about agreement and co-operation between different groups in society. They are also responsible for making political decisions, and for carrying out policies or deciding courses of action. The term 'government' refers to the group of people (the prime minister plus the other members of the cabinet) who have executive authority on behalf of society and the state.

Decisions taken by government affect you in all aspects of your life. Each year the government decides how much money should be spent on different areas. The Department of Education, for example, is allocated a sum of money to spend on

Liberty Leading the People, Delacroix, 1830.

school buildings, facilities and teachers' salaries. It must be divided between the primary, secondary and third-level sectors. These decisions determine the number of students in a classroom and the length of the school year.

The state is the whole range of public offices – the parliament, the ministers, the courts, the police, the army, the civil service and semi-state bodies – that make and enforce **collective decisions**. Since the

collective
decisions:
decisions which affect everyone in society

nineteenth century, the state has been the political entity desired by every nation of people who share a common identity, tradition, culture and language. For most of us, the state is that legally supreme but abstract entity which we defend in song, in sport, in war and in peace, and with a flag or an emblem.

Politics is the process by which society makes collective decisions which affect the whole community. Political decisions are collective decisions, affecting health care, jobs, the environment, education, sport, language, and so on. In turn, these decisions shape the kind of society in which we live, our level of unemployment and inequality, our attitude towards rape victims, for example, and our toleration of religious difference and minorities.

There is, however, no single or easy solution to any of these problems. Which decision to take can be highly contentious. It is a political decision.

Politics is too serious a business to be left to politicians.

Charles de Gaulle, President of France, 1958-1969

Politics is also the pursuit of **power**. People seeking public office wish to influence decisions, change policies or impose directives on society on behalf of the wider community, their political party, their social class or themselves. They desire the necessary clout to persuade people to reach a consensus or common view. In some circumstances, those seeking power want to coerce or force people to accept a particular point of view. People usually obtain office through election but occasionally through violence and conflict.

Sport is a political issue: Irish people opposed sporting links with South Africa, Poland and Chile in the past because of their opposition to the political regimes in those countries. Today, hare coursing is a contentious issue in Ireland. A 1993 bill to ban 'live' hare coursing was opposed by Fianna Fáil, Labour and Fine Gael. The Anti-Blood Sport campaign claims coursing is cruel to animals and should be banned. The Irish Coursing Club says it brings economic benefits to the country. They also say coursing is a traditional pastime, part of what we are. What do you think?

ASSIGNMENTS

1 Why do people seek political power?
2 How can people be coerced or forced to accept a particular point of view?
3 Is politics too serious a business to be left to politicians?
4 How do political decisions affect the world in which you live?
5 What is the difference between the state and the government?
6 Why were sporting links between Ireland and South Africa (rugby), Ireland and Poland (football), Ireland and Chile (football), opposed by some people?
7 What do we mean by the term 'political process'?

ACTIVITIES

1 Organise a classroom discussion: Many people around the world, and in Ireland, suffer from problems of unemployment, poverty, illiteracy and poor health. Others suffer from famine and disease. On the other hand some people never experience any of these problems.

(a) Is it an unfair world?

(b) Have political decisions contributed to this inequality?

(c) How would you propose to solve these problems?

2 Ask any of the third-world aid agencies for information on inequality around the world.

WHY GOVERNMENT IS ESTABLISHED

Signs of life were visible now on the beach. The sand, trembling beneath the heat-haze, concealed many figures in its miles of length; boys were making their way towards the platform through the hot, dumb sand. Three small children, no older than Johnny, appeared from startlingly close at hand where they had been gorging on fruit in the forest. A dark little boy, not much younger than Piggy, parted a tangle of undergrowth, walked on to the platform, and smiled cheerfully at everybody. More and more of them came. Taking their cue from the innocent Johnny, they sat down on the fallen palm trunks and waited. Ralph continued to blow short, penetrating blasts. Piggy moved among the crowd, asking names and frowning to remember them. The children gave him the simple obedience that they had given to the men with megaphones. Some were naked and carrying their clothes; others half-naked, or more-or-less dressed, in school uniforms; grey, blue, fawn, jacketed or jerseyed. There were badges, mottoes even, stripes of colour in stockings and pullovers. Their heads clustered above the trunks in the green shade; heads brown, fair, black, chestnut, sandy, mouse-coloured; heads muttering, whispering, heads full of eyes that watched Ralph and speculated. Something was being done ...

At last Ralph ceased to blow and sat there, the conch trailing from one hand, his head bowed on his knees. As the echoes died away so did the laughter, and there was silence ...

'Where's the man with the trumpet?'

'There's no man with a trumpet. Only me.'

The boy came close and peered down at Ralph, screwing up his face as he did so. What he saw of the fair-haired boy with the creamy shell on his knees did not seem to satisfy him. He turned quickly, his black cloak circling.

'Isn't there a ship, then? ... Isn't there a man here?'

Ralph spoke to his back.

'No. We're having a meeting. Come and join us'.

'Aren't there any grown-ups?'

'No.'

Merridew sat down on a trunk and looked round the circle.

'Then we'll have to look after ourselves.'

Secure on the other side of Ralph, Piggy spoke timidly. 'That's why Ralph made a meeting. So as we can decide what to do ...'

'Shut up,' said Ralph absently. He lifted the conch. 'Seems to me we ought to have a chief to decide things.'

'A chief! A chief!'

'I ought to be chief,' said Jack with simple arrogance, 'because I'm chapter chorister and head boy. I can sing C sharp.'

'Let's have a vote.'

This toy of voting was almost as pleasing as the conch. Jack started to protest but the clamour changed from the general wish for a chief to an election by acclaim of Ralph himself. None of the boys could have found good reason for this; what intelligence had been shown was traceable to Piggy while the most obvious leader was Jack. But there was a stillness about Ralph as he sat that marked him out: there was his size, and attractive appearance; and most obscurely, yet most powerfully, there was the conch. The being that had blown that, had sat waiting for them on the platform with the delicate thing balanced on his knees, was set apart.

'Him with the shell.'

'Ralph! Ralph!'

'Let him be chief with the trumpet-thing.'

Ralph raised a hand for silence.

'All right. Who wants Jack for chief?'

With dreary obedience the choir raised their hands.

'Who wants me?'

Every hand outside the choir except Piggy's was raised immediately. Then Piggy, too, raised his hand grudgingly into the air.

Ralph counted.

'I'm chief then.'

from William Golding, *Lord of the Flies*, 1958

The origins of modern government can be traced historically from ancient Greece and Rome, through the conflicts between parliament and monarchy in mediaeval times, to the years of revolution since the late eighteenth century. Even today, people all over the world continue to struggle for what they claim is a fairer and more just form of government. During each of these periods, political thinkers, authors, philosophers and politicians have put forward different views on the purpose and form of government which should exist.

- **Thomas Hobbes** claimed that government was needed to keep order in society. Without it, individuals would constantly fight with each other and this would lead to anarchy, chaos and open warfare. He favoured an absolute monarchy as essential to keep order in society.
  (Hobbes wrote *Leviathan,* 1651.)

- **Thomas Paine** believed that government must be prevented from usurping too much power. This control of government could only happen if there were strong laws and a constitution. If government ever failed to truly represent the 'will of the people', people had the right to overthrow the government.
  (Paine wrote *Commonsense,* 1774 and *The Rights of Man,* 1791-2.)

- **Theobald Wolfe Tone** believed that government had a duty to include all types of Irishmen, Catholic, Protestant and dissenter, within its laws. He said that government was judged on the basis of how it treated its minorities – in eighteenth-century Ireland, this meant the Catholics.
  (Tone wrote *An Argument on Behalf of the Catholics of Ireland,* 1791.)

- **Mary Wollstonecraft** believed the political system must grant equal rights to men and women. Unfortunately, women were excluded from full and equal participation in the affairs of society and were relegated to marriage and 'mindless toil'. A 'true civilisation' was one in which women were fully emancipated.
  (Wollstonecraft wrote *Vindication of the Rights of Woman,* 1793.)

- **Karl Marx** believed a new kind of society, called communism, was required to eliminate all forms of inequality based on social class. He pointed out that government actually existed to defend and protect the interests of the most powerful and wealthy in society. The poor and the working class were unable to bring about any redistribution of wealth or goods in society because they had no influence on government or laws.
  (Marx's most famous books are *The Communist Manifesto,* 1848, which he co-wrote with Frederick Engels, and *Capital,* 1867.)

ASSIGNMENTS

1 Read *Lord of the Flies* or look at the film. Discuss these issues:
   (a) Why do you think Golding chooses to tell the story through the eyes of young boys?
   (b) Why is Piggy picked out?
   (c) Does society mistreat people who are different or appear weak?
   (d) Why was Ralph chosen as the 'chief'?
   (e) What is Golding telling us about human nature? Does he believe that people are basically evil or good, competitive or collective, aggressive or mild-mannered?
   (f) Imagine yourself as the leader. How would you cope with the problem of being suddenly stranded on an island with no food or shelter? What decisions would you take?

2 Look at the ideas of Hobbes, Paine, Tone, Wollstonecraft and Marx on page 30.
   (a) Do they share any ideas in common? List them.
   (b) Which ideas and people would be opposed to each other?
   (c) Which set of ideas do you agree with **most**?
   (d) Which set of ideas do you agree with **least**?

3 What do you think is the purpose of government?

ACTIVITIES

1 Organise a classroom discussion: Thomas Hobbes believed that we are each other's enemy while Thomas Paine believed that we can live peacefully together. Who do you think is right? Which is the 'realist' and which is the 'idealist'?

2 Notice that Paine, Tone and Wollstonecraft lived at the same time.
   Paine and Tone even met. Can you find any other information about these people?

WHAT IS A DEMOCRACY?

Democracy is a very old word but its meaning has always been complex. There is no single text or writer explaining it. There is no blueprint. It has evolved over centuries through the struggle of ordinary people against powerful people.

The word **'democracy'** comes from the Greek *demos* meaning 'people', and *kratien* meaning 'to rule'. This means that the authority to govern comes from the people. Rule by the people is also contained in the phrase 'popular sovereignty' – the people are sovereign or rulers.

Michael Collins

Government of the people, by the people, for the people …

Abraham Lincoln,
The Gettysburg Address, 1863

We ordain that the elected representatives of the Irish people alone have power to make laws binding on the people of Ireland, and that the Irish parliament is the only parliament to which that people will give its allegiance …
Irish Declaration of Independence, 1919

To emphasise this point, many constitutions contain the phrase 'we the people'. In a democracy, a government governs only in accordance with rules and regulations laid down by the people through the constitution. To exceed these guidelines would make the action unconstitutional and hence illegal.

… We the people of Éire … Do hereby adopt, enact, and give to ourselves this constitution.
Bunreacht na hÉireann, 1937

In the past, few governments called themselves 'democratic'. The experiences of ancient Greek and Roman city-states were exceptions. Most regimes derived their 'authority' from wealth, custom, godliness, coercion or fear. Power was held by a tiny unelected and unrepresentative minority or by forceful individuals. The American (1776) and French (1789) Revolutions ushered in a new era.

democracy:

a form of government in which authority is exercised by the people

The four basic characteristics of a democracy are as follows:

- **the rule of law:** the power and activity of government is firmly restricted or limited by a legal relationship between the government and the governed
- **popular sovereignty/popular representation:** government is regularly elected to represent the people who have the authority or power to decide who governs
- **free, universal and equal suffrage:** the entire adult population has the same right to vote regardless of wealth, social status, religion, race, gender or mental and physical capacity, in secret and without intimidation or fear
- **individual liberty:** legal freedoms of speech, conscience, assembly, the press, and freedom from arbitrary arrest and imprisonment are enshrined in law and are protected.

The 'ideal' form of democracy is where everyone participates directly in making decisions about their community or society, for example, by a showing of hands. In the Greek 'city-states', citizens came together to vote on public issues. Later examples were the Swiss 'canton' system and the New England (USA) 'town-hall meeting' of the nineteenth century where the entire community met to make decisions.

Direct democracy is, however, considered too awkward and difficult when there are large numbers of people involved. Instead, people elect *representatives* to act and vote on their behalf. This is known as **indirect** or **representative democracy**. Today, most states and organisations operate by citizens or members electing others to represent them in parliament or on committees.

indirect or representative democracy:

a form of democracy in which people do not participate directly in making decisions but elect representatives to act on their behalf

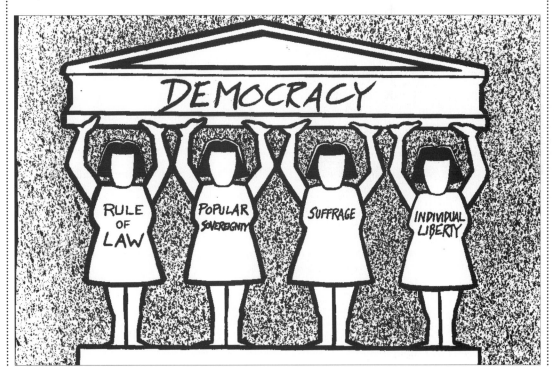

ASSIGNMENTS

1   Write a definition of the following terms in your own words: democracy, popular sovereignty, authority, universal and equal suffrage, individual liberty.

2   Review the four characteristics of a democracy.
   (a) Which characteristic do you think is the **most** important?
   (b) Which characteristic do you think is the **least** important?
   (c) Can a society call itself democratic if any of these characteristics are missing?

3   Are people always equal? Should there be special laws protecting particular groups, such as travellers or people with disability? Would this be fair on the rest of society?

4   Should people advocating racial hatred or violence be allowed the freedom to express their point of view?

5   The Irish constitution limits 'equality before the law' to 'citizens' only. Which groups of people would not be included? Do you agree with this? Why or why not?

6   Should people who have left the country (emigrated) have the right to vote?

7   Who has exercised the most power over you in your life: parents, teachers, advertisers, religious leaders?

8   What is the 'ideal' form of democracy? What is meant by 'direct democracy'?

9   What do you think Abraham Lincoln meant when he said 'Government of the people, by the people, for the people'?

ACTIVITIES

1   Organise a classroom debate: That the right to vote should be limited to:
   (a) people over 30 years of age
   (b) people who pass an examination which shows their knowledge of the economy and government
   (c) people who have never been imprisoned
   (d) people who can read and write
   (e) taxpayers.

2   Organise a classroom discussion: What is the difference between political equality and economic equality? Is one more important than the other?

PLURALISM

pluralism:
a form of rule in which many people and interests are involved in making decisions

'Rule by the people' usually means accepting the majority opinion. But how is this accomplished? How is it measured? What about minority viewpoints?

Throughout the nineteenth century, groups of people sharing a common history, identity and language desired to have their own government. France, Italy, the United Kingdom and Germany emerged in this way. Each of these states brought together, and occasionally suppressed, many linguistic and ethnic minorities in order to form one large 'nation-state' under a single government, legal and banking system, and army.

The world, however, has become increasingly more complex since then.

As a result of emigration, travel, international business and commercial activity, the influence of the media, and the spread of information, today's societies are more likely to be multi-racial, multi-ethnic and multi-religious. People have become much more aware of their individuality, their ethnic roots, their dialect, and their desire to live as they wish. They want their government to appreciate these characteristics and recognise that they are making a positive contribution to society.

Pluralism is the recognition that society is made up of many different people, of varied racial, religious and ethnic backgrounds, sexual orientation, and physical and mental ability. A pluralist democracy is one that tolerates difference. It recognises and values this diversity of viewpoints and experience.

Pluralism aims to include everyone in the decision-making process by making sure that government is not controlled by a single group of powerful individuals or elites. It aims to guard against what is called the 'tyranny of the majority'.

Majorities can sometimes dominate and do harm to society as a whole. One example is Northern Ireland. The history of the Northern Ireland state shows what can happen when a simple arithmetical formula is used to determine the majority. Under the Stormont government (1922-1972), the majority Protestant population used elections and constituency boundaries to discriminate against Catholics. **Gerrymandering** was common.

Gerrymandering:
Politicians are said to gerrymander when they establish constituency boundaries that aim to favour their supporters. The word originates from Elbridge Gerry, who, as governor of Massachusetts in 1812, divided a county into two constituencies to the advantage of the ruling Republican Party.

The 'first past the post' voting system ensured that the candidate with the most votes (the majority) could win. This made it very difficult for the minority Catholic nationalist population to ever win sufficient votes.

In the Republic of Ireland, there has also been much talk of pluralism. An over-whelming majority of the population are Catholic but some people believe that the laws and moral values of Irish society should more fairly reflect the great diversity of Irish society.

A Catholic country or its government, where there is a very substantial Catholic ethos and consensus, should not feel it necessary to apologise that its legal system, constitutional or statutory, reflects Catholic values. Such a legal system may sometimes be represented as offensive to minorities, but the rights of a minority are not more sacred than the rights of the majority.
attributed to Archbishop Dermot Ryan, 1984

We have created here something which the northern Protestants find unacceptable – a state which is itself sectarian in the acutely sectarian way Northern Ireland was in which Catholics were repressed. I believe we must tackle aspects of our constitutional laws which represent an impediment to the establishment here of a pluralist society.

Garret FitzGerald, 1981

Another example of majority domination occurred in the United States. In many southern states, people were refused the right to vote until 1970 unless they passed a literacy test or paid a 'poll tax'. This law was used to discriminate against black people who were usually illiterate or very poor.

Other countries denied women the right to vote; Switzerland had such laws until 1971.

ASSIGNMENTS

1 How can government make sure that it fairly and equally represents the interests of everyone in a multi-racial, multi-ethnic and multi-religious society?

2 In what ways do people express their individuality?

3 Should society prevent the majority from misusing its size? How can this be done?

4 Should any groups of people in society be banned? List them. Why you think so?

5 When John F. Kennedy was running for president in 1960, he was asked whether his Catholic views would influence his political decisions.
He replied: 'I am the Democratic Party candidate for President of the United States who happens to be a Catholic. I am not the Catholic candidate for President.' What do you think JFK meant by this remark?

6 Some European states have large and distinct ethnic groups.
Can you name them? Which of these groups are campaigning for separate or regional government?

THE STRUGGLE TO ESTABLISH DEMOCRACY AROUND THE WORLD

The pursuit of the four characteristics of democracy began in earnest in the eighteenth century. Before that, the dominant regime in Europe was the monarchy which had little or no responsibility to parliament. Many of the founding fathers of the American colonies had fled religious persecution and stringent commercial regulations in England. The origins of democracy occurred side-by-side with the emergence and rise of capitalism as the primary economic system throughout the world.

A new property-owning class of manufacturers arose during the industrial revolution, 1760-1830s, across Europe. They were opposed to the old ways of feudalism, which kept power and privilege in the hands of the few. They did not want power to be held by an absolute monarchy. They benefited from the creation of a new political system with basic freedoms of speech and conscience. They helped lay down the principles of modern government:

- constitutional law
- separation of powers
- checks and balances
- popular sovereignty and representation
- frequent elections.

The full democratisation of society came later. At first, the right to vote was given only to male heads of households. Later, the system of giving property-owners multiple votes was ended. Universal **man**hood suffrage (right to vote) only recognised the male's right to vote.

Female suffrage was won only after a long campaign by women's organisations during and after World War I. Discriminatory practices have continued to be used throughout the world to prevent particular racial, ethnic or religious groups from voting. The 'free vote' exists only in those states where the right to vote is not interfered with by coercion, threats or intimidation.

In the twentieth century, revolution provided the only opportunity for people to overthrow absolutist and colonial regimes. The Russian (1917) and Chinese (1949) revolutions created an alternative model of society, based on the collective good – to ensure economic prosperity for all and not just the wealthy few. Communist states provided a short-lived but impressive level of economic and social benefit for its citizens.

After four hundred years of colonialism and exploitation by many European nations, the people of Africa, Asia, the Middle East and South America fought and achieved

their independence. Their individual paths to democracy have not been smooth. Many continue to be plagued by tribal, ethnic and political conflict caused by poverty and inequality, economic under-development, huge debt and rapid population growth.

In many instances, the military or wealthy elites have seized power. Some regimes are noted for their suppression of human and civil rights, the use of arbitrary and authoritarian power, and vast inequalities of wealth among the population. Power has often been controlled by a single political party which can be extremely repressive and authoritarian. Ruling elites have used their public positions to amass great fortunes for themselves and their families. The rise of

Islamic fundamentalism has created a new form of authoritarian regime.

In rare instances, the monarchy has played a liberating role. In 1975 King Juan Carlos of Spain came to power after the death of General Franco, the last remaining post World War II fascist leader. The king played a key role in establishing liberal democracy in Spain, and in putting down a military coup in 1981.

India is known as the world's largest democracy because it has a population of over 700 million people. It won its independence from Britain in 1949. Its constitution has similarities to the Irish constitution. South Africa began its transition to democracy when it held its first all-race elections in April 1994.

THE STRUGGLE TO ESTABLISH DEMOCRACY IN IRELAND

Early Irish society was ruled by a small group of kings and nobles. The status of commoners was determined by whether they owned any property, while women did not count.

The Norman invasions of 1169 inaugurated a new phase of Irish statehood. The lordship or lord lieutenant of Ireland was the king's personal representative. He was advised by a 'privy council' composed of officials and occasionally by the 'great council' or parliament.

The Irish parliament first met in Castledermot, Co. Kildare in 1264. Over the next four centuries, it came to resemble the English parliament. It had a House of Commons with 300 elected members, and a House of Lords with members from the Church of Ireland and the landed gentry.

The Act of Union, 1800, formally united Ireland with the other members of the United Kingdom – Wales, Scotland and England – and abolished the Irish parliament. One hundred Irish representatives were elected instead to seats in the House of Commons (Westminster) while thirty-two members of the Church of Ireland and peers sat in the Lords.

Under the Union, the lord lieutenant held executive authority in Ireland. His chief secretary was in charge of the day-to-day running of the government's affairs. The lord lieutenant's official residence was the Viceregal Lodge in the Phoenix Park. In 1937, it became Áras an Úachtaráin, the house now occupied by the President of Ireland.

Free, universal and equal suffrage was granted slowly:
- to Catholics in 1793
- to landholders in 1829
- to householders and lodgers in 1884
- to all men, and some women over 30 years in 1918
- to all adults over 21 years in 1922
- to all adults over 18 years in 1972.

Throughout the nineteenth century, Irish nationalists fought for independence. They campaigned for a Home Rule Bill but Ulster unionists were opposed to this. The Government of Ireland Act, 1920, provided

Parnell carves out a nation.

for the establishment of two parliaments. Nationalists rejected the partitioning of Ireland and pursued a war of independence. The Anglo-Irish Treaty was signed between Britain and Ireland in July 1921.

Many of the 'founding fathers' of the new Irish state were professionals, teachers and journalists. James Larkin, leader of the Irish Transport and General Workers' Union, played an important role in the 1913 Dublin Lock-Out but not in the 1916 Rising. However, another great trade unionist James Connolly was executed for his role as a leader of the **Irish Citizen Army**.

Women such as Louie Bennett, Helena Moloney, Delia Larkin and Hannah Sheehy Skeffington were also prominent in the trade union, nationalist and suffrage movements of the time. Constance Markievicz became a member of the government of the First Dáil. As Minister for Labour, she was the first female member of any government anywhere in the world.

The new independent state was known as Saorstát Éireann. It had jurisdiction over twenty-six of the thirty-two counties of Ireland. Under the terms of the treaty, Ireland's written constitution reflected the principles of other liberal democratic governments: limited government, popular sovereignty, universal suffrage, and protection of individual liberty. Particular attention was given to protecting the rights of the Protestant minority.

A new constitution, *Bunreacht na hÉireann*, was introduced in 1937. In 1948, Ireland became a republic.

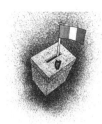

Irish Citizen Army: *a working-class organisation founded in 1913 and under the influence of James Connolly, it sought to bring about a socialist revolution in Ireland*

RESEARCH ACTIVITIES

1   Write a short essay on the role played by one of the following in the democratisation of Irish society: Wolfe Tone, Daniel O'Connell, Thomas Davis, Charles Stewart Parnell, James Connolly, Hannah Sheehy Skeffington, Constance Markievicz, Louie Bennett.

2   Using the characteristics of a democracy listed on page 33, find out in what years member states of the European Union became 'democratic'?

3   Which nation states are controlled today by:
    (a) military regimes?
    (b) powerful elites?
    (c) single-party governments?
    (d) religious elites?

4   Many third-world countries have found the transition to democracy very difficult. Elections are held but the problems of poverty and economic inequality remain. Collect material from one of the third-world aid agencies about the difficulties experienced by people striving for democracy in these countries.

5   Watch the film *Gandhi* (dir. Attenborough). Did India find the transition to an independent democracy difficult? What role did Gandhi play in this transition?

IS THERE AN ALTERNATIVE TO DEMOCRACY?

liberal democracy:

a form of democracy with strong regard for individual rights

Ireland is a liberal democracy. This is the most common form of political system in the developed world. We usually refer to it simply as democracy.

A **liberal democracy** combines the features of both liberalism and democracy. These are the principles of individual rights (liberalism) and government of and by the people (democracy).

A *non-liberal society* believes that the needs of society as a whole are more important than the needs of an individual; that collective good is superior to individual rights. For instance, in such a society, a person would not have the right to claim personal custody over mineral wealth found on his or her land. It would be viewed as a national resource. An example of a non-liberal society would be the former communist states of eastern and central Europe.

A *non-democratic society* does not believe that the government should be responsible to the people or that it should continually seek re-election to office. It believes that when people have too much say in how society is run, the result is confusion and chaos. It believes a strong government is required to get things done. Fascist regimes are anti-democratic.

Many supporters of democracy are, however, often critical of it. The most common criticisms are:

- Even though everyone has a vote, the poor and unemployed have little influence. Political equality is not the same as economic equality.
- Politicians are often so anxious to ensure their own re-election that they make foolish and reckless promises.

English fans give the fascist salute at the Ireland versus England football match in Dublin 1995.

A   G U I D E   T O   I R I S H   P O L I T I C S

Some people are critical of all forms of government. They are anarchists. Their ideal community is one in which there are absolutely no restrictions on individuals. Self-governing communities – without government and laws – are considered the best form of society. Anarchists are often called libertarian socialists because of their strong defence of individual freedom.

Can society exist without any form of government and law?

Respect for the liberty of others is not a natural impulse with most men ... If all men's actions were wholly unchecked by external authority ... the strong would oppress the weak, or the majority would oppress the minority, or the lovers of violence would oppress the more peaceable people ...

from Bertrand Russell, *Proposed Roads to Freedom: Socialism, Anarchism and Syndicalism*, 1919

ASSIGNMENTS

1 Read again the extract from Bertrand Russell above.
   (a) Why does he believe that some kind of government and law is always necessary?
   (b) What does he think is likely to happen without laws?
   (c) William Golding's story, *Lord of the Flies,* which was discussed at the beginning of this chapter, outlines a situation that could develop when there is no law or government. How does that story compare with Russell's view?
2 Some states forbid membership of, or recognition to, fascist, communist or paramilitary organisations.
   (a) Can you name any that do?
   (b) Do you agree with banning these organisations?
3 Write either for or against the motion: That it is important to vote.
4 The following comment was overheard during an election campaign:
   'If I don't vote, it won't affect me.' Is this person right? What do you think?

ACTIVITY

Organise a classroom discussion:
(a) Are there any circumstances in which you would favour:
   – a non-liberal political system?
   – a non-democratic political system?
(b) 'Democracy works best when people participate.'
   How do you think you can get involved?
(c) In periods of economic or political crisis, should the government be given extra power to make any necessary decisions?
(d) Is there an alternative to democracy?

42

C H A P T E R   3

POLITICAL FOUNDATIONS

THE NEED TO LIMIT POWER

At the Meeting on … Sunday the question of whether or not to begin work on the windmill was to be put to the vote. When the animals had assembled in the big barn, Snowball stood up and … set forth his reasons for advocating the building of the windmill.

Then Napoleon stood up to reply. He said very quietly that the windmill was nonsense and that he advised nobody to vote for it. Then he promptly sat down again; he had spoken for barely thirty seconds, and seemed almost indifferent as to the effect he produced.

At this Snowball sprang to his feet, and, shouting down the sheep who had begun bleating again, broke into a passionate appeal in favour of the windmill. Until now the animals had been about equally divided in their sympathies, but in a moment Snowball's eloquence had carried them away …

… Napoleon stood up and, casting a peculiar sidelong look at Snowball, uttered a high-pitched whimper of a kind no one had ever heard him utter before.

At this there was a terrible baying sound outside, and nine enormous dogs wearing brass-studded collars came bounding into the barn. They dashed straight for Snowball, who only sprang from his place just in time to escape their snapping jaws … all the animals crowded through the door to watch the chase …

… Silent and terrified, the animals crept back into the barn. In a moment the dogs came bounding back. At first no one had been able to imagine where these creatures came from, but the problem was soon solved: they were the puppies whom Napoleon had taken away from their mothers and reared privately. Though not yet full-grown, they were huge dogs, and as fierce-looking as wolves. They kept close to Napoleon. It was noticed that they wagged their tails to him in the same way as the other dogs had been used to do to Mr Jones.

Napoleon, with the dogs following him, now

mounted on to the raised portion of the floor where Major had previously stood to deliver his speech. He announced that from now on the Sunday morning Meetings would come to an end. They were unnecessary, he said, and wasted time. In future all questions relating to the working of the farm would be settled by a special committee of pigs, presided over by himself. These would meet in private and afterwards communicate their decisions to the others. The animals would still assemble on Sunday mornings to salute the flag, sing 'Beasts of England', and receive their orders for the week; but there would be no more debates …

from George Orwell, *Animal Farm*, 1945

In the decades and centuries before the American (1776) and French (1789) Revolutions, kings, tsars, emperors, princes, noble families and tribal leaders reigned supreme. Their right to rule was usually based upon birthright, military might, wealth or claims of godliness. They ruled by decree, demanding complete and unquestioning loyalty and obedience. Anyone standing up to them would often face harsh imprisonment or death. Terms such as 'dictatorship' or 'tyranny' are used to describe such arbitrary and overwhelming use of power.

The Greek city-states (8th–5th c. BC) and the Roman Republic (6th–1st c. BC) were notable exceptions. Under these 'republics', laws were introduced which restricted the power of nobles, and citizens were encouraged to participate in public assemblies and the legal process. People elected their own officials to represent them. Eventually, the widening gap between rich and poor led to conflict and political breakdown.

The word **'republic'** comes from the Latin words *res publica*, meaning public thing or affair. It refers to a form of government where elected officials rather than kings have the power to rule. In an absolute monarchy, kings and queens claim the right to rule because of their royal blood or claims of godliness.

Another important milestone on the road to democracy was the civil war in England in 1642. It was caused by increasing tension between Charles I and parliament. The establishment of the commonwealth and protectorate under Oliver Cromwell, 1649-1660, attempted to limit the authority of the monarchy and to assert the power of parliament. The *Bill of Rights* (1689), like the *Magna Carta* (1215), were key documents limiting royal power.

The origins of modern republicanism are to be found in the American Revolution and the French Revolution. Supporters of both revolutions questioned the existence of the monarchy and its authority. They represented victories for the rights of citizens over the complete power of monarchy. They fought for the right to shape their own destiny by voting and electing their own government.

The French *Declaration of the Rights of Man and of the Citizen* (1789) and the American *Declaration of Independence* (1776) proclaimed that all people, as individual human beings, have basic rights of citizenship. These are the right to 'life, liberty and the pursuit of happiness'. To safeguard these rights, the abuse of power by government must be curtailed by law.

republic: *a form of government in which authority rests with the people and not with monarchs or dictators*

RESEARCH ACTIVITIES

1 Look up the following terms in your dictionary: autocracy, oligarchy, theocracy. Write a definition in your own words.
2 Can you name any rulers who claimed power on the basis of birthright, military might, wealth or claims of godliness?
3 People often use the word 'dictatorship' to describe someone with absolute power. Which rulers would you put in this category?
4 Read George Orwell's *Animal Farm* (1945) or Jonathan Swift's *Gulliver's Travels* (1726). Each story appears to be an adventure but is actually a criticism of people in power. Swift criticised the English government of the 18th century while Orwell was critical of the rise of communism.
    (a) What is happening in the story?
    (b) What criticism is the author making of those who hold power?
    (c) What do you think the moral of the story is?

WHY DO WE HAVE A CONSTITUTION?

Ms Caroline Maher from Artane, Dublin arriving with her father Mr. Martin Maher at the polling station at Scoil Eanna, Artane, Dublin before her marriage.

constitution:

set of rules and fundamental principles according to which a society, organisation or state is governed

The people involved in the historical events we have just discussed strongly believed that power would be abused unless there were clear rules to limit the power of government.

These rules of government are incorporated in a **constitution**. They regulate the power and authority of the government. They prevent political leaders from abusing power or making decisions arbitrarily. This is known as the principle of 'limited government'.

Constitutions also accept the principle of 'popular sovereignty'. This is the belief that the people are the real rulers in society. They elect a government to represent them. If the government abuses power or rules without their support, then people have the right to choose another government. A constitution is the single most important document of any state. It is the basic law of the state.

The functions of a constitution are:

- to declare political principles stating the aims and values of the society
- to indicate under whose authority the constitution was enacted, establishing the principle of popular sovereignty
- to define the duties of the state – protecting the common or general good
- to describe the rules regulating government activity making sure that government cannot abuse its authority
- to guarantee popular participation setting out how elections to public office will take place
- to protect citizens' rights guaranteeing personal liberty, freedom of speech and religion, and equality before the law
- to provide a procedure for amendments allowing for changes to the constitution.

The different functions of a constitution are usually grouped together in consecutively numbered Articles. Each part of an Article is called a Section or Sub-Section. Article 41.3.2 of the Irish constitution, for example, is read as: Article 41, Section 3, Subsection 2.

The Preamble is the introduction which usually contains a statement of political ideals. Citizens' rights are often grouped together and called human or personal rights.

We hold these truths to be self-evident, that all men are created equal, that they are endowed by their Creator with certain unalienable rights, that among these are Life, Liberty and the Pursuit of Happiness. That to secure these rights, governments are instituted among men, deriving their just powers from the consent of the governed.

That whenever any form of government becomes destructive of these ends, it is the right of the people to alter or to abolish it, and to institute new government, laying its foundations on such principles and organising its powers in such form, as to them shall seem most likely to effect their safety and happiness.

American Declaration of Independence, 1776

All powers of government ... derive, under God, from the people whose right it is to designate the rulers of the state and, in final appeal, to decide all questions of national policy, according to the requirements of the common good. These powers of government are exercisable only by or on the authority of the organs of state established by this constitution.

Article 6, *Bunreacht na hÉireann*

Protest outside the Dáil by the Parent's Association for People with a Mental Handicap.

ASSIGNMENTS

1   Why do some people believe that government should be answerable or accountable to the people? What is this principle called?

2   Constitutions promote the principles of 'limited government' and 'popular sovereignty'. Underline the words in the extracts from the American *Declaration of Independence* (1776) and the Irish constitution, Bunreacht na hÉireann, (1937) on page 48, which describe these principles.

3   Below are passages from *Bunreacht na hÉireann*.
    Match these passages with the appropriate constitutional function listed on page 47.

    (a) 'And seeking to promote the common good, with due observance of Prudence, Justice and Charity, so that the dignity and freedom of the individual may be assured, true social order attained, the unity of our country restored, and concord established with other nations ...'

    (b) 'We, the people of Éire ... do hereby adopt, enact, and give to ourselves this constitution.'

    (c) '[The] powers of government are exercisable only by or on the authority of the organs of state established by this constitution.'

    (d) 'The state guarantees liberty for the exercise of the following rights, subject to public order and morality: the right of citizens to express freely their convictions and opinions ...'

    (e) 'The state pledges itself to safeguard with especial care the economic interests of the weaker sections of the community, and, where necessary, to contribute to the support of the infirm, the widow, the orphan, and the aged.'

    (f) 'Any provision of this constitution may be amended, whether by way of variation, addition, or repeal, in the manner provided by this Article.'

    (g) 'Every citizen without distinction of sex who has reached the age of eighteen years ... shall have the right to vote at an election for members of Dáil Éireann.'

RESEARCH ACTIVITY

Youth and sports clubs, farmers' organisations, trades unions and student unions also have constitutions. Examine the constitution of a local organisation:

    (a) What are the aims of the organisation?
    (b) Who is the membership?
    (c) How are decisions taken and by whom?
    (d) How often are elections held?

ACTIVITY

Organise a classroom debate: That the power of government should not be limited.

RIGHTS OF INDIVIDUALS

'LIFE, LIBERTY AND THE PURSUIT OF HAPPINESS'

Another way to limit the power of government is to protect the rights of individuals. Many constitutions safeguard individual or human rights. Government cannot deny or restrict these rights. They include:

- the right to practise the religion of one's choice
- the right to express one's opinion freely
- the right to choose one's own government
- the right to personal liberty
- the right to be treated equally before the law
- the right to own property.

The American constitution guaranteed these rights in its first ten amendments, known as the 'Bill of Rights'. Both *Poblacht na hÉireann* (1919) and the 'Fundamental Rights' section of *Bunreacht na hÉireann* (1937) include some of these rights. Today, human rights are endorsed in many international documents:

- United Nations Universal Declaration of Human Rights
- European Convention on Human Rights
- Inter-American Convention on Human Rights
- African Charter on Human and People's Rights
- International Covenant on Civil and Political Rights
- International Covenant on Economic, Social and Cultural Rights.

Ireland is a signatory to several of these documents. Groups like Amnesty International, the Red Cross, the United Nations Human Rights Committee, and the Human Rights Commission act as international watch-dogs for human rights violations.

The Irish Republic guarantees religious and civil liberty, equal rights and equal opportunities to all its citizens, and declares its resolve to pursue the happiness and prosperity of the whole nation and of all its parts, cherishing all the children of the nation equally, and oblivious of the differences carefully fostered by an alien government, which have divided a minority from the majority in the past …

Poblacht na hÉireann, 1919

- *Congress shall make no law respecting an establishment of religion ... or abridging the freedom of speech, or of the press ...*
- *... the right of the people to keep and bear arms, shall not be infringed ...*
- *No soldier shall be ... quartered ... but in a manner to be prescribed by law.*
- *The right of the people to be secure in their persons, houses, against unreasonable searches and seizures shall not be violated ...*
- *No person shall ... be deprived of life, liberty, or property, without due process of law ...*
- *In all criminal prosecutions, the accused shall enjoy the right to a speedy and public trial ...*
- *... the right of trial by jury shall be preserved ...*
- *Excessive bail shall not be required ... nor cruel and unusual punishments inflicted.*
- *... rights shall [be] retained by the people ...*
- *... powers ... are retained to the States ... or to the people.*

Bill of Rights, Constitution of the United States of America, 1787

ASSIGNMENTS

1 Examine the extract from *Poblacht na hÉireann* on page 50. Underline what you think are the most important phrases in this extract.

2 Which rights are guaranteed by the Bill of Rights in the American constitution? Name them.

3 Which human rights do you think are most important? Are there any circumstances in which you think it might be appropriate for government to restrict these rights?

RESEARCH ACTIVITIES

1 Collect information from groups such as Amnesty International or the Red Cross. What human rights violations do these groups claim occur in countries around the world? How do these organisations act as 'watch-dogs' for human rights?

2 Invite a representative from groups such as Amnesty International or the Red Cross to talk to your class.

CONSTITUTIONS USUALLY MARK A 'NEW BEGINNING'

A constitution is usually written to indicate a break with a previous type of political system and society and the beginning of a new one:

- The USA enacted a constitution in 1787 to mark its independence from England.
- Cuba's constitution of 1959 marked its birth as a communist society after a violent revolution.
- Ireland has had three constitutions (1919, 1922, 1937), each one marking an important moment in its political development.
- Germany, Italy and Japan enacted new constitutions (1946, 1947, 1949) to mark the end of fascism after World War II.
- South Africa's constitution of 1994 marked the birth of a multi-racial government.

BUNREACHT NA hÉIREANN
(CONSTITUTION OF IRELAND)

IRISH CONSTITUTIONAL HISTORY

To codify:

To arrange laws in a systematic collection

reland has had three constitutions.

- Constitution of Dáil Éireann, (*Poblacht na hÉireann*), 1919
- Constitution of the Irish Free State (*Saorstát Éireann*), 1922
- Constitution of Ireland (*Bunreacht na hÉireann*), 1937

All Irish constitutions, like most constitutions, have been written or **codified**. The United Kingdom does not have a constitution. The powers of the monarchy and the government are limited by a combination of legal documents and conventions. Laws can be passed to make changes, whereas the Irish must have a referendum to amend the constitution. The rights of British citizens are guaranteed by law, not by a constitution.

CONSTITUTION OF DÁIL ÉIREANN (*POBLACHT NA hÉIREANN*), 1919

In the general election of November 1918, Sinn Féin won 73 out of 105 seats. Instead of taking seats in Westminster, Sinn Féin representatives established their own independent parliament, Dáil Éireann. A meeting was held in Dublin's Mansion House in January 1919. A *Declaration of Independence* proclaimed the birth of the Irish Republic. The participants also adopted a constitution which described the rules of the First Dáil.

This constitution was a short document of five Articles. It provided for a government and a parliament, how the Dáil would work, how funds could be raised, and procedures for amendment.

The government was made up of a president or head of government and four other ministers. Together they formed a cabinet which held 'executive power'. The Dáil was the 'legislature'.

The *Democratic Programme* acted as a Preamble to the constitution. It declared 'the right of the people of Ireland to the

First Dáil meeting at the Mansion House, Dublin

ownership of Ireland' and stressed the Irish Republic's commitment to democracy and equality. This document was written by Seán T. O'Kelly.

An earlier version, written by Thomas Johnson of the Irish Labour Party, was a far more radical document. It supported co-operatives and the removal of all inequality in society based on social class.

We declare in the words of the Irish Republican Proclamation the right of the people of Ireland to the ownership of Ireland, and to the unfettered control of Irish destinies to be indefeasible, and … we declare that the nation's sovereignty extends not only to all men and women of the nation, but to all its material possessions, the nation's soil and all its resources, all the wealth and all the wealth-producing processes within the nation, and … we reaffirm that all right to private property must be subordinated to the public right and welfare.

We declare that we desire our country to be ruled in accordance with the principles of Liberty, Equality, and Justice for all, which alone can secure permanence of Government in the willing adhesion of the people.

We affirm the duty of every man and woman to give allegiance and service to the Commonwealth, and declare it is the duty of the Nation to assure that every citizen shall have the opportunity to spend his or her strength and faculties in the services of the people …

It shall be the first duty of the government of the Republic to make provision for the physical, mental and spiritual well-being of the children, to secure that no child shall suffer hunger or cold from lack of food, clothing, or shelter, but that all shall be provided with the means and facilities requisite for their proper education and training as citizens of a free and Gaelic Ireland …

Democratic Programme of Dáil Éireann

ASSIGNMENTS

Read the extract from the *Democratic Programme*.

1 Find and underline the following words in the text: equality, allegiance, sovereignty, liberty, indefeasible, commonwealth. Using your dictionary, write a definition for each of the words.

2 What do you think the following quotes mean?
   (a) 'the right of the people of Ireland to the ownership of Ireland'
   (b) 'the right to private property must be subordinated to the public right and welfare'
   (c) 'the principles of Liberty, Equality, and Justice for all'
   (d) 'the duty of every man and woman to give allegiance and service to the commonwealth'
   (e) 'first duty of the government of the Republic to make provision for the physical, mental and spiritual well-being of the children …'
   (f) 'citizens of a free and Gaelic Ireland'.

ACTIVITY

Organise a classroom debate: That the ideals and aspirations of the *Democratic Programme* are still important.

CONSTITUTION OF THE IRISH FREE STATE (*SAORSTÁT ÉIREANN*), 1922

Despite the proclamation of an Irish Republic in 1919, the British remained in Ireland. The war of independence, 1919-21, attempted to defeat them by military force. This war was brought to an end with the truce of 11 July, 1921 and the Anglo-Irish Treaty of 6 December, 1921.

Disagreement over the terms of the treaty and whether it should be accepted led to a bitter civil war (1922-23). Éamon de Valera opposed the treaty because it failed to grant full independence to the entire island of Ireland. Michael Collins advocated acceptance of the treaty because he saw it as a step on the road to full independence. The treaty was ultimately passed by the Dáil: 64 voters in favour to 57 against.

The provisional government, the predecessor to the Irish Free State, came into existence on 14 January, 1922.

William T. Cosgrave became leader of the pro-treaty wing of Sinn Féin. It changed its name to Cumann na nGaedheal and to Fine Gael in 1933. De Valera and his anti-treaty supporters retained the name Sinn Féin until 1926 when he left to form Fianna Fáil.

The *Constitution of the Irish Free State* created a sovereign or independent, self-governing state within the British commonwealth – an association of former British colonies. This meant that all decisions taken by the Irish government, parliament or courts could be subject to the greater interests of the commonwealth. The constitution also contained many unique features of self-rule, upheld secularism, and provided basic protection for the Protestant minority.

Statue of Queen Victoria being removed from the Leinster House lawn.

55

As a member of the British commonwealth:
- Irish citizens were subjects of the king of England
- Dáil members were required to pledge an oath of allegiance to the king
- the governor general was the king's representative in Ireland. He had the power to **veto** legislation passed by the Dáil
- Ireland could be required to participate in a war involving other commonwealth states
- decisions of the Irish Supreme Court could be overturned by the privy council of the House of Lords.

As a new, self-governing state:
- citizens could propose legislation to the Dáil
- citizens could vote by 'referendum' for laws or constitutional amendments
- a lower tier of ministers, known as 'extern' ministers, could be elected by the Dáil
- the state could not support any religion or discriminate on the basis of religious belief
- children were guaranteed free primary education
- nominations to Seanad Éireann should have 'special regard' to minority representation.

By 1936, many of these sections had been removed by a series of amendments.

veto:
the power to reject

Garda officer speaking to British Army Officer as recruits wait to enter Dublin Castle, 1922.

ASSIGNMENTS
1 Look back over this chapter. What do you think the following concepts mean: popular sovereignty, secularism, minority representation?
2 What were the main differences between those who supported the treaty and those who did not?
3 If you could propose legislation, which issues would you choose?
4 Éamon de Valera did not want to take the oath of allegiance in order to take his seat in the Dáil after the 1927 election. How did he manage this?

CONSTITUTION OF IRELAND *(BUNREACHT NA hÉIREANN)*, 1937

King Edward VIII's abdication from the British throne in 1936 provided the opportunity for a new constitution to be introduced in Ireland. Éamon de Valera had been the leading opponent of the treaty and the *Constitution of the Irish Free State*. After the general election of 1932, which his Fianna Fáil party won, he began dismantling all symbols of commonwealth status from the constitution.

Éamon de Valera
- appointed a token governor-general and gradually stripped him of powers
- questioned the authority of the privy council
- abolished the Seanad in 1936.

Bunreacht na hÉireann is known as Éamon de Valera's constitution because of his influence on, and supervision of, its framing. It represented both a formal and a symbolic separation from Britain. Its endorsement of liberal democratic principles, nationalist aspirations and Catholic ethos signalled the emergence of a truly Irish state.

The constitution introduced a number of significant changes. Its principal features were the following:

- the principle of popular sovereignty is endorsed
- the moral authority of God as the ultimate power is recognised
- the Oireachtas is established as the national parliament with supreme law-making authority
- people have the right to challenge the constitutionality of any law in the High and Supreme Courts
- citizens' personal and civil rights are guaranteed
- a claim to the 'whole island of Ireland' is expressed
- the Catholic Church is granted a 'special position' – this was removed in 1972
- Catholic social teaching with respect to the role and the status of the family is embraced
- the constitution can be changed by amendment and referendum.

ACTIVITIES

1   Organise a classroom discussion: What do the following extracts from *Bunreacht na hÉireann* mean?
    (a) 'The national territory consists of the whole island of Ireland, its islands and the territorial seas.' (Article 2)
    (b) 'All citizens shall, as human persons, be held equal before the law.' (Article 40.1)
    (c) 'The right of the citizens to express freely their convictions and opinions ...' (Article 40.6.1.i)
    (d) 'In particular, the state recognises that by her life within the home, a woman gives to the state a support without which the common good cannot be achieved.' (Article 41.2.1)

(e) The state pledges itself to safeguard with especial care the economic interests of the weaker sections of the community, and, where necessary, to contribute to the support of the infirm, the widow, the orphan, and the aged.' (Article 45.4.1)

(f) 'We, the people of Éire, Humbly acknowledging all our obligations to our Divine Lord, Jesus Christ, Who sustained our fathers through centuries of trial ... (Preamble).

2 How do the aspirations stated in passages (b), (c), (d) and (e) above affect your life?

3 Why do you think unionists living in Northern Ireland find the claim in (a) above offensive?

4 Some people feel that the view expressed in the Preamble (f) represents a particular religious view. What do you think?

CONTROVERSY AND DEBATE

Many sections of the constitution have raised controversy over the years. An all-party Commission on the Constitution in 1966 recommended removal of the special status of the Roman Catholic Church and alteration of Articles 2 and 3 on national unity.

There have been thirteen **amendments** to *Bunreacht na hÉireann*. These have included the lowering of the voting age to 18 years, membership of the European Community, and a ban on abortion.

Some of the amendments have involved changes in wording, while others did not raise much public interest or debate. However, several amendments have had a dramatic effect on the shape and direction of the country:

- 3rd (1972) Accepted membership of the European Community (Art. 29.4)
- 4th (1972) Lowered voting age to 18 years (Art. 16.1)
- 5th (1972) Deleted 'special position' of the Catholic Church (Art. 44.1)
- 8th (1984) Inserted 'right to life for the unborn' into a new section (Art. 40.3.3)
- 9th (1984) Extended voting rights in Dáil elections to other citizens of the European community (Art. 16.1)
- 10th (1987) Authorised Irish state to ratify the Single European Act (Art. 29.4)
- 11th (1992) Authorised Irish state to ratify the Maastricht Treaty forming the European Union (Art. 29.4)
- 12th (1992) Inserted the 'right to travel' section to permit women to travel outside the country for an abortion (Art. 40.3.3)
- 13th (1992) Inserted 'right to information' section to permit distribution of abortion information under law (Art. 40.3.3).

amendments:
to make changes or alter the wording of a constitution or legislation

NATIONAL ASPIRATIONS

NATIONAL TERRITORY

Article 2 of the constitution defines the national territory as the 'whole island of Ireland, its islands and the territorial seas'. Article 3 asserts the right of the Republic to jurisdiction over the entire island of Ireland.

These aspirational claims have been highly contentious. Unionists argue that these sections represent a territorial claim over Northern Ireland, which is part of the United Kingdom. For others, these sections state a commitment to unify the island of Ireland.

In 1990 the Irish Supreme Court ruled that the government must actively seek to unify the Irish national territory in order to comply with the constitution. The court said there was a 'constitutional imperative' in this matter. If the government failed to act, it would be behaving unconstitutionally. This is known as McGimpsey v Ireland.

The Joint Declaration on Northern Ireland, 1993 and the Framework Document, 1995, recognised that Northern Ireland was part of the United Kingdom

John Major and John Bruton.

until the majority there decide otherwise.

In the negotiations on the future of Northern Ireland, these articles will be altered to remove the Republic's territorial claim on Northern Ireland.

STATEHOOD

To the surprise of many people at the time, *Bunreacht na hÉireann* did not proclaim Ireland to be a republic. Instead, 'Éire' is a 'sovereign, independent, democratic state' (Article 4). The Republic of Ireland Act was introduced in 1948, and Ireland was recognised as a Republic in 1949.

CHURCH-STATE RELATIONS

The arena of church-state relations has provided some of the most heated public debates in contemporary Irish society. The constitution reflects the religious values of the overwhelming majority of its Catholic citizens.

Many people believe that the constitution should represent all citizens and not just the majority. They have campaigned for the separation of church and state. They have campaigned for the wide availability of contraceptives, for divorce, for sex education in schools, and for non-religious control of schools. Some have also argued that in order to bring about reconciliation between nationalists and unionists, the Republic should not be seen to endorse any particular religion.

The 'special position' of the Holy Catholic Apostolic and Roman Church in Article 44 was deleted from the constitution in 1972. The state now guarantees 'freedom of conscience and the free profession and practice of religion ...'. The Preamble still retains a declaration favouring the Christian tradition. Article 6 claims the 'powers of government ... derive, under God'.

Articles 41, 42 and 43 are concerned with the family, education and ownership of property. These sections have also been controversial because, as Professor Basil Chubb says, they are 'obviously Catholic in content and tone' (1982).

THE POSITION OF WOMEN

EQUALITY

In 1937, women were the major critics of the new constitution. They believed that it failed to give adequate protection to the rights of all citizens. A proposal that equality 'before the law' should be 'without distinction of sex' was not considered necessary (Article 40.1).

Article 41.2 uses the words 'woman' and 'mothers' interchangeably, citing their 'life within the home' and 'duties to the home'. It appears that women are relegated to the home while no mention is made of men or fathers in relation to the home.

This constitutional recognition of women's work within the home has, however, been recently cited to support the idea that women working in the home should be paid or given some economic protection.

Women's right to sit on juries, to receive equal pay and social welfare payments, and to half the family home are some of the important legal cases that have arisen since the 1970s.

ABORTION

The inclusion of a provision in Article 40.3.3 protecting the equal rights of the unborn has proven to be very controversial.

Despite laws banning abortion in Ireland, many people saw the need to protect the 'life of the unborn' while many others argued that abortion was an important option for pregnant women in difficult medical and psychological circumstances. The debate surrounding the 8th Amendment in 1984 resurfaced in 1992, following the pregnancy of a 14-year-old who had been raped. A case came to be known as 'the X case' because the names of those involved were withheld.

To resolve the constitutional issues arising from 'the X case', the government proposed three constitutional amendments to Art. 40.3.3. A referendum was held in November 1992. The 12th and 13th amendments permit the distribution of abortion information and freedom to travel outside the country, for an abortion. A proposal for abortion in limited circumstances was not passed.

THE FAMILY

Articles 41 and 42 grant special rights to the family. These are said to be 'inalienable and imprescriptable rights, antecedent and superior to all positive law'. This means that the family has a moral authority which cannot be altered by people. Therefore, Article 41.3 prohibits 'the dissolution of marriage, on which the family is founded'. Under this section, divorce is not permitted.

Prior to 1927, only wealthy people could obtain a divorce by appealing to the Senate and then to the privy council of the House of Lords. Since then, there has never been any provision for divorce in Ireland.

In recent years, public opinion polls have shown a high number of people favouring divorce. Yet, when an amendment to repeal the ban was put to a referendum in 1986, it failed. Why? At that time, some people disagreed with the requirement to divide family property between the husband and wife. Also, many women felt they would be left impoverished if the husband divorced and remarried.

Since then, the government has introduced laws to provide for legal separation for married couples who have been living apart, and to divide family property. Another referendum on divorce is pending.

PRIVATE PROPERTY

Article 43 of *Bunreacht na hÉireann* provides extensive protection to the owners of private property. The history of the struggle for, and control over, land is very closely tied up with the struggle for independence from Britain. The constitution states that the right of ownership must, however, be regulated by the 'principles of social justice'.

Derrynaflan chalice

It is often very difficult to reconcile the rights of the individual to own property and the rights of the community. Several court cases have attempted to resolve some of the issues. For example, a man and his son found the Derrynaflan Chalice in a bog on their land. Was the chalice a private or a national treasure? The Supreme Court ruled that the state could have the chalice after compensation was paid to the finders.

NATIONAL SOVEREIGNTY

Ireland's entry into the European Community, and the extension of community authority under the Single European Act and the Maastricht Treaty required amendments to Article 29 in 1972, 1987 and 1992. Public concern has been expressed over the way European law often takes priority over Irish domestic law.

Irish neutrality is an issue of particular concern. Since World War II, the Irish government has pursued a policy of being neutral in international conflicts. It has refused to join any military alliance, such as **NATO** or the **WEU**. Irish membership of the United Nations has involved participation in UN peacekeeping forces in the Lebanon, Bosnia and Somalia.

Under the terms of the Maastricht Treaty, the European Union countries will begin to frame a common defence and security policy which may include the formation of a European Army. There is opposition to this idea in Ireland, although many people believe that Ireland can no longer remain neutral in the face of conflict elsewhere in Europe, for example in Bosnia.

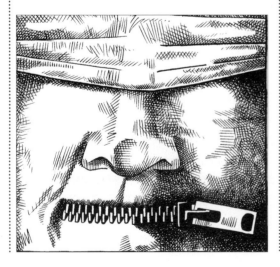

CIVIL LIBERTIES

The Irish constitution guarantees personal rights to all citizens under Article 40. The state may also choose to limit these rights in order to maintain public order and protect public morality.

Bunreacht na hÉireann 'guarantees' the following rights:
1. that all citizens are equal before the law
2. that a citizen's personal and property rights shall be upheld
3. citizen's personal liberty shall not be taken away
4. 'dwelling of every citizen is inviolable'
5. that every citizen may 'express freely their convictions and opinions'
6. that every citizen is free 'to assemble peaceably and without arms'
7. that every citizen is free 'to form associations and unions'.

CENSORSHIP

Censorship is permissible if what is published, heard or seen is considered to be 'blasphemous, seditious or indecent'. It is also allowed if what is expressed either publicly, on the radio, in the press, in the cinema or in publication can threaten the security, morality or authority of the state.

The issue of censorship has focused most often on broadcasting. The 1960 Broadcasting Act, which established RTE, makes clear that nothing can be broadcast, either on television or on radio, that might be 'likely to promote, or incite to, crime or would tend to undermine the authority of the state ...'. When the current conflict in Northern Ireland began in 1968, Section 31 of this legislation prohibited the appearance

NATO and WEU:
Both NATO and the WEU are military alliances. NATO or the North Atlantic Treaty Organisation includes many European countries, the USA and Canada as members. The WEU or Western European Union includes most west European countries. Since Ireland is neutral, it is not a member of either organisation.

of, or interviews with, anyone from a named (proscribed) loyalist or nationalist paramilitary organisation.

Irish and international concern was consistently expressed about Section 31 because it was viewed as a form of censorship – in other words, a way to remove from the airwaves views that the government did not like. Questions of individual rights to freedom of information and access to information were raised by many groups, including Amnesty International and the United Nations Committee on Human Rights. In January 1994, Section 31 was allowed to lapse.

James Joyce

Censorship of film and publications have existed since the 1920s. Legislation established a Censor and the Censorship Board whose function it is to oversee the sale and distribution of films, books, magazines, etc. which are considered 'indecent', 'obscene' or 'blasphemous'. Publications or films intended for general release, in paperback and in English were more likely to be censored than those for private showings, in hard back or in the Irish language.

Works by many of Ireland's and the world's most famous writers have been banned at one time or another, from Irish bookshelves and libraries: Austin Clarke, Noel Coward, Barbara Cartland, Graham Greene, James Joyce, Ernest Hemingway, Aldous Huxley, Walter Macken, Simone de Beauvoir, Seán O'Casey, Seán O'Faolain, Liam O'Flaherty and Jean Paul Satre among others. Many films and information on contraception and abortion have also been restricted.

PERSONAL LIBERTY

The constitution allows the government to introduce emergency legislation. Under Article 28.3.3, a state of emergency can be declared during a time of war or other threat to the security of the state. Under this declaration, internment or other restrictions on people's personal liberty can be introduced.

A state of emergency was first declared in Ireland in 1939 during World War II. It was known as The Emergency. This lasted until 1976. Another state of emergency was then immediately introduced because of increased terrorist activity arising from the conflict in Northern Ireland. This state of emergency was in operation until 1995.

ASSIGNMENTS

1 Which article of the constitution expresses an 'aspiration' or desire for unity of the island of Ireland?

2 Do you think it is accurate to describe *Bunreacht na hÉireann* as expressing Catholic social and moral values?

3 Why were women among the major critics of the Irish constitution?

4 Why is divorce prohibited in Ireland?

5 The right of an individual to own property can interfere with the rights of the community. Can you think of any circumstances when this can happen?

6 What does it mean for Ireland to be neutral in international conflicts? Are you in favour of this? Would you agree with the formation of a European army which Irish men and women would join?

7 The Irish constitution guarantees personal rights to all citizens. Which rights do you think should be guaranteed under any constitution?

8 Should the constitution guarantee special protection for women or minority groups in society?

9 Censorship is permitted under the constitution if what is published, heard or seen is considered to be 'blasphemous, seditious or indecent'. What do the words 'blasphemous, seditious or indecent' mean? What kind of material could be censored under the constitution?

10 Do you think censorship should exist? Is there any kind of material you believe should not be allowed: pornography? abortion information? material promoting or portraying violence, racism, anti-semitism or terrorism?

RESEARCH ACTIVITY

Use the newspaper collection in your local library. Look up information on the background to one of the topics discussed on pages 58-63 and write a report on the issues involved. What is your opinion?

ACTIVITY

Organise a classroom debate on one of the following topics:

(a) That the aspiration for Irish unity is no longer practicable.

(b) That Ireland should remain neutral.

(c) That women's position within the home should be guaranteed.

(d) That the rights of private ownership should be limited.

(e) That censorship is never permissible in a democratic society.

CENTRAL
GOVERNMENT

TYPES OF GOVERNMENT

The word 'government' can have two meanings. Firstly, we talk about 'the government', meaning the holders of 'office'. These are the men and women who form the political executive of the state, with full responsibility for the management of public affairs. Secondly, the word 'government' is used more generally to refer to the structure of government, how the system itself works. This chapter is concerned with the second meaning of the word.

There are two basic types of freely-elected government: the parliamentary model and the presidential model. With the exception of the former communist states and France, all other European states have a parliamentary model of government. The United States of America is the prime example of a presidential type of government.

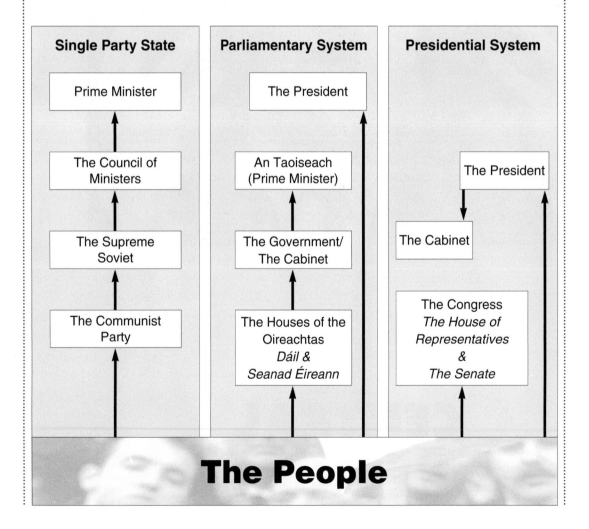

Single Party State

Prime Minister

↑

The Council of Ministers

↑

The Supreme Soviet

↑

The Communist Party

↑

Parliamentary System

The President

An Taoiseach (Prime Minister)

↑

The Government/ The Cabinet

↑

The Houses of the Oireachtas
Dáil & Seanad Éireann

↑

Presidential System

The President

↓

The Cabinet

↑

The Congress
The House of Representatives
&
The Senate

↑

The People

PARLIAMENTARY GOVERNMENT

The parliamentary form of government evolved over centuries in England. The basic principles and ideals for this type of government, which have been adapted around the world, are as follows:

- the parliament has supreme law-making authority
- the prime minister is elected by the parliament at its first meeting after a general election
- the cabinet is appointed by the prime minister
- the prime minister is the chief executive or chairperson of the cabinet of ministers
- the government is responsible to the parliament
- the head of state is a formal position, separate from the day-to-day running of government.

Ireland is a parliamentary democracy. The Taoiseach is the Irish prime minister. The Tánaiste is the deputy prime minister and the parliament is called the Oireachtas. This structure of government follows very closely upon the British 'Westminster' model, also known as the cabinet government model.

PRESIDENTIAL GOVERNMENT

In this form of government, the president is both the head of government and the head of state. The main features of the US presidential model are as follows:

- the president is directly elected by the people
- the president is accountable to the people, not to the legislature (parliament)
- the president is both the political executive and the head of state
- each branch of the state (the executive, the legislature and the judiciary) has separate and distinct powers
- the president can be impeached or removed from office.

The American President is directly elected every four years. Once elected, the president appoints a cabinet. Unlike our system, members of the US cabinet are not allowed to be members of parliament, called the Congress. In addition, the president appoints several thousand members of the White House staff which advise on all issues of government. Although the president does not participate in the law-making process, he or she influences the decisions taken by the legislature and uses the media to influence the public.

The legislature is known as the Congress. It is more powerful than Ireland's Oireachtas. It has much greater authority to make laws and investigate issues of national importance. It conducted impeachment proceedings against President Richard Nixon who was forced to resign in 1973.

The US judiciary has had significant influence over legislation and in defence of individual rights. Individuals, groups, states of the US, and the national government can all bring cases to the US Supreme Court to decide if a law is unconstitutional. The judiciary has played a major role in restricting capital punishment, prohibiting racial discrimination, allowing abortion and protecting the right of journalists to keep their sources confidential.

France has a form of presidential government, sometimes called semi-presidential. It was introduced by Charles de Gaulle in 1958. Political power is shared between the prime minister, who is the  head of the cabinet, and the president, who has the real power. The president is directly elected for a seven-year term. The French president has more power than the American president.

ASSIGNMENTS

1   What are the two meanings of the word 'government'?
2   Complete the following sentence in your own words:
    The power of the government must be limited because ...
3   What is the other name for a 'cabinet government'?
4   Why do we use the word 'Westminster' to describe the cabinet form of government?

RESEARCH ACTIVITIES

1   Use your daily newspaper to find examples of the following:
    (a) recent actions which show the power of the American president
    (b) recent actions which show how the Taoiseach is responsible to the Dáil.
2   List countries which have
    (a) a parliamentary system of government,
    (b) a presidential system of government.
3   In Ireland, the president is the head of state. Who is the head of state in Britain?
    Who are the heads of state of the other members of the European Union?
4   Choose one of the following political leaders of the twentieth century.
    Why is this person famous? What contribution did he or she make to their country or to world politics? How important do you think his or her contribution was?
    Winston Churchill (UK), Adolf Hitler (Germany), Franklin Delano Roosevelt (USA), John Fitzgerald Kennedy (USA), Richard Nixon (USA), Ronald Reagan (USA), Margaret Thatcher (UK), General Francisco Franco (Spain), Julius Nyrere (Tanzania), Charles de Gaulle (France), Alexander Dubcek (Czechoslovakia), Lech Walesa (Poland), Col. Quadafi (Libya), Jomo Kenyatta (Kenya), Indira Gandhi (India), Pol Pot (Cambodia), Juan Peron (Argentina), Daniel Ortega (Nicaragua), General Augusto Pinochet (Chile), Benito Mussolini (Italy).

COMMUNIST GOVERNMENT

Communist states have a system of government which resembles the parliamentary system. The former USSR (Union of Soviet Socialist Republics or Soviet Union) had a prime minister (premier), a cabinet (council of ministers), and a parliament (Supreme Soviet). The Supreme Soviet was directly elected every five years. A constitution set out the rules and guidelines of government activity and power.

In practice, power was held by the communist party. It was organised like the state with a general secretary, central committee, and the party congress (or conference). It ensured that only candidates approved by it were elected and only laws meeting its approval were passed.

Leaders like Lenin (USSR), Mao (China), Hoxha (Albania), Castro (Cuba), Tito (Yugoslavia), Kim Il Sung (North Korea) and Ho Chi Min (Vietnam) were seen as heroes. A personality cult grew up around them; their speeches were put into books and taught to schoolchildren.

However, massive changes to the political and economic systems, known as **glasnost** and **perestroika**, were introduced by Mikhail Gorbachev in the USSR between 1985-91. These changes were so dramatic that they led to the collapse of the political system in the USSR.

These changes also had a knock-on effect throughout central and eastern Europe. Communist states began to transform themselves into liberal-democratic societies. East Germany reunited with west Germany, Czechoslovakia was divided into the Czech Republic and Slovakia, and Yugoslavia broke up into six different states (Serbia, Herzegovina, Montenegro, Bosnia, Croatia and Macedonia). Today, few communist states remain. Cuba, North Korea, China and Vietnam are examples.

glasnost:

the Russian word meaning 'openness', it refers to the policy introduced by Gorbachev promoting honest and open discussion of public issues in the Soviet Union

perestroika:

the Russian word meaning 'reconstruction', it refers to the policy introduced by Gorbachev advocating wide ranging changes in the political and economic system in the Soviet Union

---

RESEARCH ACTIVITIES

1   Look up information on the role played by Mikhail Gorbachev in the political and economic changes in the USSR during the 1980s.
2   What are the names of the new independent states formed from the former USSR?
3   Look up information on one of the following people: Vladimir Lenin (USSR), Mao Zedong (China), Enver Hoxha (Albania), Fidel Castro (Cuba), Josi Tito (Yugoslavia), Kim Il Sung (North Korea), Ho Chi Min (Vietnam), Joseph Stalin (USSR), Boris Yeltsin (USSR).

LIBERAL DEMOCRACY

We learned in the last two chapters that constitutions were devised to limit the power of government and protect the rights of individuals. How government is organised can also achieve these aims.

All liberal-democratic governments share the following three principles in common.

- **Checks and balances**

  Power is also distributed between these institutions. The government might propose a new law, but only the legislature can pass a bill into law, and the judiciary might rule that the law is unconstitutional.

- **Bicameralism**

  The word bicameralism means that the legislature is also divided between two houses or chambers: an upper house and a lower house. Each house has specific powers.

- **Separation of powers**

  Jobs are divided between several institutions, each of which has very specific powers: government has executive power, the legislature makes the laws, and the judiciary has the power of judicial review.

THE IRISH PARLIAMENTARY SYSTEM OF GOVERNMENT

Ireland has a tiered system of decision-making. This means that different decisions are made at different levels. Until 1972, there were two tiers: national decision-making centred around the Oireachtas and the cabinet, and local or community decision-making was based upon local authorities and city managers. Since Ireland entered the European Community, now known as the European Union or EU, many decisions affecting Ireland are taken by the Council of Ministers, the European Commission or the European Parliament.

In Ireland, power is shared between the government, the Oireachtas, and the High and Supreme Courts. There is also the civil service and the army. This complicated system of 'checks and balances' prevents any one of these institutions from becoming too strong and misusing its power. If one of these institutions acts outside its duties it would cause a constitutional crisis.

ASSIGNMENTS

1　What are the three tiers of Irish political decision-making?
2　In Ireland, the Dáil is the lower house and the Seanad is the upper house. Which are the upper and lower houses in the British parliament?
3　Which other countries have a bicameral legislature? Give two examples.

THE OIREACHTAS

The Oireachtas is the Irish parliament. It is located in Leinster House, Kildare Street, Dublin 2. The building, originally known as Kildare House, was built between 1745-1747 as the town residence of James Fitzgerald, Viscount Molesworth and Earl of Kildare. It was sold to the Royal Dublin Society (RDS) in 1815. In 1924, it was acquired by the Irish Free State.

The Oireachtas is divided into two 'houses': the Dáil (House of Representatives) and Seanad (Senate). The Dáil and the Seanad:

- discuss government proposals
- pass bills to become laws
- evaluate and comment on government business
- remove the president or a judge of the Supreme or High Court
- declare a state of emergency.

According to the constitution, the Dáil has more responsibilities than the Seanad, and has power over the Seanad. This is because the Dáil is popularly elected and is considered to be more in touch with the people. The Dáil:

- approves financial receipts, expenditures and the budget
- initiates all constitutional amendments
- elects the Taoiseach and cabinet ministers
- approves of international agreements
- has the power to declare war
- may limit the Seanad's debating time.

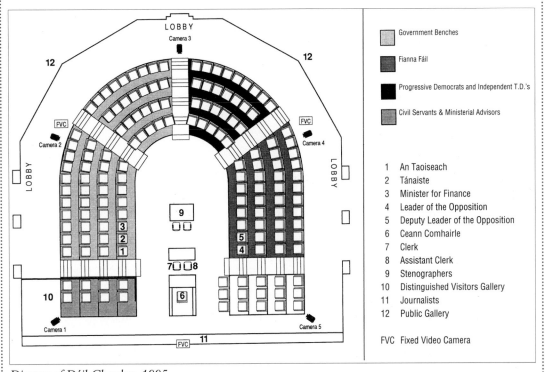

Government Benches

Fianna Fáil

Progressive Democrats and Independent T.D.'s

Civil Servants & Ministerial Advisors

1 An Taoiseach
2 Tánaiste
3 Minister for Finance
4 Leader of the Opposition
5 Deputy Leader of the Opposition
6 Ceann Comhairle
7 Clerk
8 Assistant Clerk
9 Stenographers
10 Distinguished Visitors Gallery
11 Journalists
12 Public Gallery

FVC Fixed Video Camera

Diagram of Dáil Chamber, 1995.

The Seanad has limited powers. It cannot challenge or veto decisions of the Dáil or of the government.

The Seanad can only:

- debate legislation
- amend legislation
- discuss motions.

There are 166 members of the Dáil, known as Teachtaí Dála (TD). Each TD represents approximately every 20,000 electors in a constituency. Elections take place at least once every five years.

The Seanad has 60 members known as senators. They are elected in three different ways:

- forty-three are elected by a combination of local government councillors, out-going senators and in-coming TDs
- six are elected by university graduates

Eamon de Buitléar, film director and environmentalist who was appointed to the Seanad, 1989–92.

- eleven are nominated directly by the Taoiseach.

This electoral system ensures that the Seanad always has a majority which represents the government party.

ASSIGNMENTS

1 Can you name the two houses of the Oireachtas?
2 Why is the Dáil considered to be more in touch with the people than the Seanad is?

RESEARCH ACTIVITIES

1 In which constituency do you live? Name the TDs who represent your constituency.
2 Find an example from the daily newspaper or the radio/television news to illustrate each of the functions of the Dáil and Seanad.
3 Write to your local TD. Ask him or her to explain what TDs do.

ACTIVITIES

1 Arrange a visit to the Dáil and to the Seanad. Write a newspaper-type report on the debate you heard. How does your report compare with the reports in the newspaper?
2 Invite a member of the Dáil and/or Seanad to your class.
  Discuss with him or her how the Dáil and Seanad work.

AN TAOISEACH

After every general election, a prime minister or Taoiseach is elected by the Dáil. The candidate or candidates for Taoiseach must be members of the Dáil. In other words, he or she must be a TD. The Taoiseach, as head of the government, is usually the leader of the majority political party in the Dáil. The Tánaiste is the deputy prime minister and often holds a senior cabinet post.

The Taoiseach has the following responsibilities:

- directs cabinet business
- makes ministerial and judicial appointments
- dissolves the cabinet
- decides the timing of a general election
- nominates eleven people to the Seanad
- opens Dáil sessions.

According to his or her ability, personality or political will, the Taoiseach either dominates, controls or simply chairs the cabinet. The political commentator Brian

John Bruton

Farrell described these styles of leadership as the difference between being a 'chairman or chief'. Whichever leadership style a Taoiseach assumes, the power to decide on Dáil business, the timing of elections and leadership of the government means that the Taoiseach has tremendous authority.

Taoisigh:

The position of Taoiseach was first introduced in the 1937 Constitution. Up until then, the position was referred to as 'President of the Executive Council'

These people have served as **Taoisigh**:

- W.T. Cosgrave (Cumann na nGaedheal), 1922-32
- Éamon de Valera (Fianna Fáil), 1932-48, 1951-54, 1957-59
- J.A. Costello (Fine Gael), 1948-51, 1954-57
- Seán Lemass (Fianna Fáil), 1959-66
- Jack Lynch (Fianna Fáil), 1966-73, 1977-79

- Liam Cosgrave (Fine Gael), 1973-77
- Charles Haughey (Fianna Fáil), 1979-81, 1982-82, 1987-92
- Garret FitzGerald (Fine Gael), 1981-82, 1982-87
- Albert Reynolds (Fianna Fáil), 1992-94
- John Bruton (Fine Gael), 1994-

THE CABINET

The Taoiseach nominates seven to fifteen TDs or senators to become members of the cabinet. They are usually TDs, but up to two Senators may be appointed. Senator James Dooge became the Minister for Foreign Affairs under Garret FitzGerald in this way between 1982 and 1987.

Each member of the cabinet is given responsibility for at least one government department at the discretion of the Taoiseach. This is called having a 'portfolio'. The Taoiseach may also be in charge of a government department. Ministers may appoint special advisors who leave office when the minister does. The Fianna Fáil/Labour Party coalition government of 1992 was the first to appoint advisors called programme managers.

Ministers of state or junior ministers are not members of the cabinet. They have special departmental responsibilities and work under a minister. For example, the Department of Education has a junior minister with specific responsibilities for youth and sport.

In the cabinet system of government, the cabinet acts as a united policy-making body. The cabinet works according to the constitutional principle of **'collective authority'**. This means that decisions taken by the cabinet are supported by every member of the cabinet and that decisions are confidential or secret. All cabinet ministers must defend decisions even if they personally disagree.

Even though the government is the political executive – that is, making and carrying out policy – it must always be responsible to the Dáil. If, for example, the government proposes a new law or a change in the taxation system, but fails to win the approval of the Dáil on the issue, it is said to have lost the 'confidence' of the Dáil and may be forced to call a general election.

THE ATTORNEY GENERAL

The attorney general is appointed by the Taoiseach as the government's legal advisor and representative in major legal proceedings.

The attorney general plays a key role in drafting new legislation. The attorney general is one of three non-cabinet members who are allowed to attend cabinet meetings; the others are the government chief whip (who has responsibility for organising Oireachtas business on behalf of the government) and the secretary to the government. On occasion junior ministers have been allowed to attend but not to vote at cabinet meetings.

collective authority:
the Irish constitution, like in the UK counterpart, maintains that every member of the cabinet is jointly responsible and accountable for every decision taken by the cabinet

---

RESEARCH ACTIVITIES

1   What are the names of the present members of the cabinet? What portfolios do they hold?

2   Who are the ministers of state? What are their responsibilities?

3   Do you think the Taoiseach should be a chairman or chief?

4   Who is the present attorney general? Can you find any examples in recent newspapers to illustrate the responsibilities of the attorney general?

5   Write a job description for one of the following;
    (a) the Taoiseach
    (b) the Minister for Education
    (c) a TD.
6   Who am I?
    (a) I was Taoiseach and so was my father
    (b) I won a number of All Ireland medals for my county (Cork) before I became
         Taoiseach
    (c) I was not leader of my party when I became Taoiseach
    (d) I was Taoiseach without winning a general election outright
    (e) I was the first Taoiseach to shake the hand of the president of Sinn Féin
    (f) I was Taoiseach before I was elected President
    (g) I was the first Taoiseach to meet the Northern Ireland prime minister
    (h) I appointed the first Junior Minister for Women's Affairs.
7   Write a short biography on one of the men who have been Taoiseach.

ACTIVITY

Organise a classroom debate: That cabinet discussions should be made public.

THE PRESIDENT

The president is the head of state and is the guardian of the constitution. This formal difference between 'state' and 'government' is typical of parliamentary systems. In Ireland, we distinguish between the 'ceremonial' leadership of the titular head of state and the 'efficient' leadership of the Taoiseach and the cabinet.

The UK, like the Netherlands and Spain, is a **constitutional monarchy**. Queen Elizabeth II is the head of state, and the prime minister is the head of the government. The USA does not distinguish between the state and the government; the president is both the head of state and the head of the government.

The 1919 Constitution of Dáil Eireann established a president of Ireland, but it was equivalent to today's Taoiseach. This was Éamon de Valera. Under the Anglo-Irish Treaty of 1921, the governor-general was the representative of the British crown in Ireland. Like his counterpart in Canada, he could withhold approval for any bill or pass it on for the king's consideration. However, these were largely symbolic functions. When Fianna Fáil was elected in 1932, de Valera effectively ignored and downgraded the office until it was finally abolished in December 1936.

Bunreacht na hÉireann formally established a separation between state and government. The president is directly

constitutional monarchy:

refers to a political system which is headed by a monarch whose authority is limited by a constitution, as in the UK, the Netherlands, Sweden or Spain

elected by the entire voting population for a seven-year term and can be re-elected only once. The president can be removed from office only by impeachment 'for stated misbehaviour' by both the Dáil and Seanad.

The president has more than a ceremonial role. The president:

(a) is guardian of the constitution

(b) formally appoints or retires members of the government

(c) must formally sign every bill into law, or may, after consulting the council of state, decline to sign a bill into law, and instead
  • refer the bill to a referendum of the people
  • refer the bill to the Supreme Court to decide whether any aspect of it raises constitutional questions

(d) is 'supreme' commander of the defence forces

(e) has the right to pardon, commute or remit punishment imposed by any court, especially in capital cases

(f) can dissolve the Dáil to allow a general election following a request from a Taoiseach who has lost the 'support of a majority'. Or, if the president feels, 'in his absolute discretion', that other political parties in the Dáil could form a government without a general election, he or she may refuse the request to dissolve the Dáil.

Every citizen over 35 years is entitled to stand for election to the presidency. He or she must be nominated by at least twenty people who are members of the Dáil or the Seanad, or by at least four county (or county borough) councils. A president who has served a term may renominate him/herself as a candidate for a second term.

There was an agreed candidate for president on five occasions: 1938, 1952, 1974, 1976 and 1983. This meant there was no election.

The presidents of Ireland have been:
Douglas Hyde, 1938–45
Seán T. O'Kelly, 1945–59
Éamon de Valera, 1959–73
Erskine Childers, 1973–74
Cearbhaill O'Dálaigh, 1974–76
Patrick Hillery, 1976–90
Mary Robinson, 1990–

Erskine Childers

THE COUNCIL OF STATE

This is an advisory group to the president. It must be convened under circumstances set out by the constitution. Its membership consists of:

- the Taoiseach, the Tánaiste, the chief justice, the president of the High Court, the Ceann Comhairle of the Dáil, the Cathaoirleach of the Senate, and the attorney general
- former presidents, Taoisigh and chief justices
- seven appointees of the president.

THE PRESIDENCY IN CONTROVERSY: THE RESIGNATION OF CEARBHAILL Ó DÁLAIGH

In 1976, there was a large increase in paramilitary violence in the Republic and in Northern Ireland, committed by the IRA (Irish Republican Army) and the UFF (Ulster Freedom Fighters). A Fine Gael senator had been assassinated in 1974 and the British ambassador in 1976, two no-warning bombs went off in Dublin and Monaghan killing twenty-eight people, and there were two IRA hunger-strikes in Portlaoise Prison, 1975 and 1977.

The Fine Gael/ Labour Party coalition government introduced two bills designed to give the police, army and courts additional powers to tackle terrorist threats. A state of emergency was declared. Emergency legislation restricted people's rights. Fianna Fáil and the Irish Council for Civil Liberties claimed that the proposals were unconstitutional because they

Cearbhaill Ó Dálaigh

restricted 'personal liberty' or freedom to move about.

After consulting the council of state, President Cearbhaill Ó Dálaigh exercised his rights under the constitution to refer the proposals to the Supreme Court. The Supreme Court decided they were constitutional because a state of emergency had been declared.

Further controversy arose when the Minister for Defence, Patrick Donegan, criticised the president's decision. Addressing a group of army officers, he said the decision 'was a thundering disgrace ... The fact is that the army must stand behind the state'.

This provoked a constitutional crisis for three reasons. Firstly, by his remarks, Donegan was seen to over-step the constitutional boundary between government and state. He had interfered with the discretionary powers of the president to refer bills to the Supreme Court. Secondly, as Minister for Defence, Donegan criticised the president in front of army officers of whom the president is commander-in-chief. Thirdly, Donegan's comments suggested that the president did not stand behind the state.

President Ó Dálaigh felt that the minister's comments were contemptuous. He believed the minister should resign to restore constitutional credibility to the office of the president. The Taoiseach, Liam Cosgrave (Fine Gael), neither sought nor supported Donegan's resignation. Although Donegan did eventually apologise, President Ó Dálaigh felt the apology was inadequate and he resigned.

Patrick Hillery (Fianna Fáil) was the Irish member of the European Commission at the time. He agreed to return to Ireland and stand unopposed for president. Given the controversy, neither Fine Gael nor the Labour Party contested the election.

ASSIGNMENTS

1   What can a president do if she or he feels that a new law or bill may conflict with an individual's rights under the constitution?
2   The president has a group of people from whom she or he may seek advice; what is this group called?
3   The president has six different powers. Can you find an example under each heading?
4   What is the formal process by which a president is removed from office? Can you name the American president who resigned before this formal process began?
5   Why is the president the 'supreme' commander of the defence forces?

RESEARCH ACTIVITIES

1   Who am I?
   (a) I was a member of The Gaelic League and a Protestant before I became President of Ireland
   (b) My father was an Englishman, a famous writer and Republican who was assassinated during the civil war
   (c) I was the only serving president to resign from office
   (d) I was one of the chief negotiators for Ireland's entry into the EEC (EU)
   (e) I was born in America and was sentenced to death for my part in the 1916 Rising
   (f) I was the first woman to be elected President.
2   Write a job description for the president of Ireland.
3   Write a short biography of one of the presidents of Ireland.
4   Do you think the president should have more, or less, power? Why?

THE JUDICIARY

The Four Courts, Dublin.

Bunreacht na hÉireann provides for the establishment of a judicial or court system. Courts of the first instance are those which first hear a case. These are the local circuit and district courts which have limited jurisdiction or authority. Courts of final appeal are those which hear cases when either side is unhappy with a decision or verdict. These include the High and the Supreme Courts. These courts also have power of judicial review.

Judicial review is the procedure by which anyone can refer laws to the High or Supreme Court to verify its constitutionality. When a law is challenged in this way, it affects the entire population and not just the person bringing the case. This process gives the courts the ability to influence legislation and policy.

Unlike the USA, Irish people have been slow to use the courts to defend their rights. However, since 1967, the courts have assumed a more 'interpretive' role. In Ryan v Attorney General, 1960, the court recognised nine additional personal rights which were unspecified in the constitution.

They included:

- the right to bodily integrity
- the right to work, to belong to a trade union
- the right to a career
- the right to free movement
- the right to marry.

Until then the courts had limited personal rights to those mentioned in Article 40 of *Bunreacht na hÉireann* (page 62).

Some other historic cases were:

The People (Attorney General) v O'Brien (1965): the Supreme Court ruled that if the police obtain evidence, including a confession, during their investigation of a crime in a manner which infringes a person's rights, the evidence cannot be used to convict the person. In 1990, the Gardaí were not allowed to produce drugs found during the search of a suspect's flat because the search warrant was invalid.

McGee v Attorney General (1974): the Supreme Court ruled that persons could import artificial contraceptives for their own use. A number of gradual changes in the law over the years has resulted in the widespread availability of artificial contraceptives.

De Burca v Attorney General (1976): the Surpeme Court ruled that everyone, including tenants in private and local authority dwellings and women, had the right to sit on juries. The Juries Act 1976 granted the right to serve on juries to all citizens between 18-70 years who are registered to vote at Dáil elections.

Norris v Attorney General (1984): the Supreme Court ruled that Irish law could outlaw homosexuality. This decision was over-ruled by the Court of Human Rights in Strasbourg. It found that Ireland failed to recognise the right to sexual privacy as stated in the *European Convention of Human Rights*. As a result the law was changed in 1993. Homosexuality was decriminalised, and 17 years was established as the common age of consent for sexual activity by both sexes.

THE CIVIL SERVICE

The job of running a modern state and providing services to the entire population requires a tremendous amount of administration and organisation. As societies have grown, their demands and needs expanded, the importance and influence of the civil service has likewise grown. This huge administrative network is often called the bureaucracy of a state.

The word bureaucracy can often be derogatory. It can suggest inefficiency or red-tape, and the civil servants can be seen as faceless bureaucrats. To a public seeking advice or benefits, the often inexplicable number of forms to be filled in, different buildings to visit or people to speak with, can make the system seem unnecessarily unfriendly and complicated.

Civil servants are expected to be politically neutral and non-party, and to give the same level of service and commitment to every government. In contrast, each new US president makes thousands of appointments throughout the civil service, the White House and Congress.

The relationship between government ministers and civil servants can be complicated. The British television comedy series 'Yes Minister' showed a minister interested only in furthering his career and a civil servant determined to preserve his influence. Who is really in charge?

Government ministers make important policy decisions with the advice of senior civil servants. In turn, civil servants can have a significant influence over ministers particularly when they are preparing advice, briefing documents and policy initiatives. But politicians must ultimately bear the political cost of decisions. If unpopular or bad decisions are taken, they could lose their ministerial office or seat in the next election.

The civil service:
• advises the government on policy
• identifies aims and priorities of policy
• administers and implements decisions.

Government departments were first set up by the Ministries and Secretaries Act, 1924. Over the years, government functions have been reorganised, new departments formed and others renamed. An incoming government may decide to reorganise or rename the departments, based upon its own political priorities.

There is a hierarchy of ministerial posts. The Minister of Finance is the most important after the Taoiseach and Tánaiste. The power and influence of the Department of Finance comes from the fact that it controls the spending and earning of money throughout the state. It can decide if another department or minister may or may not spend money on particular projects – hospitals, schools, industrial development, etc. Refusal to allocate sufficient funds to a project is often politically unpopular.

GOVERNMENT DEPARTMENTS

Agriculture and Food: responsible for agriculture and food-related industries. It promotes disease eradication and control programmes, and is also concerned with EU schemes, regulations and grants. It ensures the quality of agricultural produce both for the domestic and export markets.

Arts, Culture and the Gaeltacht: concerned with the economic development of Gaeltacht areas and with the development of relevant cultural and social policy. It also seeks to promote the use of Irish as a first language. This department now has responsibility for broadcasting policy, the promotion of artistic and cultural activities, and national image.

Defence and the Marine: responsible for the administration of the defence forces including recruitment and equipment purchase, and it plans and co-ordinates civil defence measures. It is also responsible for the planning of activities relating to fisheries, aquaculture and fish-processing. Shipping policy, search and rescue, and research and development, are some of the other areas that come under its domain.

Education: administers public education at first and second level, and special education. It also handles state funding granted to third-level institutions, curriculum development, and assessment procedures, including the junior and leaving certificates.

Enterprise and Employment: responsible for manpower policy, industrial relations and working conditions. Training schemes are run under FÁS and CERT. It also monitors industrial disputes and processes applications to and claims from the European Social Fund. It has the major task of job creation, particularly through the Industrial Authority (IDA) and the promotion of indigenous industry.

Environment: oversees the activities of local authorities – housing, planning, environmental matters, pollution control, water and sewerage schemes, roads, driver-testing and vehicle registration.

Equality and Law Reform: responsible for reforming existing statutes and proposing new legislation. It is also intended to protect the rights of the disabled, women, travellers and other groups which may encounter discrimination.

Finance: responsible for government finances. It must ensure that there is sufficient money to meet all requirements and oversee its proper expenditure which is organised through the annual Budget.

Foreign Affairs: advises on foreign relations and represents Irish policy in Northern Ireland and foreign countries. It is informed on matters of international law and protects Irish citizens abroad.

Health: exercises control over all the regional health boards, reviews existing services and proposes future services. It also runs health education services for the public.

Justice: responsible for the administration of courts, prisons and policing. It is also concerned with land registry, controls licensing of intoxicating liquor, gaming and lotteries, and has responsibility for the censorship of films and publications.

Social Welfare: administers social insurance and welfare schemes within the state social security system.

Taoiseach: provides administrative services to the government and to the business of the Taoiseach. It is responsible for a range of national agencies, including the National Economic and Social Council.

Transport, Energy and Communications: responsible for the major semi-state companies, and policies connected with travel, by air, rail and road. It is also responsible for energy policy, the forest service, for the exploration and development of natural resources, and the postal and telecommunications systems.

Tourism and Trade: responsible for the development of industrial policy, international trade agreements and regulation, company and patents law, merger control and consumer protection. The promotion of tourism is also part of its brief.

RESEARCH ACTIVITIES

1   Some information about the government departments is listed above.
    Find out more detailed information for each department.
    Give some examples of the work they do.
2   Name the ministers in charge of each department.
3   Which departments have ministers of state? Name the minister of state in each post.
4   What are semi-state bodies? Name some of them and their functions.
    Which department is in charge of each of them?

THE DEFENCE FORCES

In many societies, the military plays a crucial role in politics. In some cases, it poses a constant threat to civilian governments; in others, it has assumed power in circumstances of political instability. Military coups have been commonplace in many parts of the world: south and central America, Africa and Asia. But the military have also seized power in developed democratic societies.

The capture of power in 1967 by the generals in Greece ushered in a six-year period of harsh, authoritarian rule. Opposition politicians, trade unionists and civil rights workers were imprisoned or assassinated. In contrast, a military coup in Portugal in 1974 played a key role in transforming that society into a democracy following the death of the fascist leader, Premier Antonio Salazar. Portuguese colonies of Angola and Mozambique were liberated. General elections were held in 1976.

In the USA, the military has a great deal of influence over policy, although it has never sought political power. The Pentagon is a huge organisation, employing thousands of people. Its influence extends beyond the operations of the defence forces to include foreign policy, space exploration, technological research and development, and intelligence surveillance. Like other organised and powerful groups in society, the military wants the government to adopt policies which are favourable to its interests. A cynic might say that the pursuit of peace would not be in the military's favour.

In Ireland, the defence forces have had

83

little influence on political affairs. Even in 1932, the army stayed neutral despite fears to the contrary by Fianna Fáil. Indeed, when entering the Dáil for the first time, it is said that some members of FF carried pistols because they feared the army would prevent Éamon de Valera assuming office. No such event occurred.

Today the defence forces primarily assist the Gardaí in domestic security: patrolling the border between Northern Ireland and the Republic of Ireland, mounting checkpoints, escorting cash, carrying out search operations against terrorist and drug activities, and fishery protection.

During World War II, Ireland remained neutral. Since then, there has been little threat of foreign invasion. In recent years, the Irish military has increased its participation in United Nations peace-keeping efforts. Irish military participation in a European defence force or army may evolve through our membership of the EU.

HOW THE PARLIAMENTARY SYSTEM WORKS

Following a general election, all elected TDs meet to form a government. If a single party has a majority of the 166 TDs it will be able to elect a Taoiseach and form a government. If no party has a majority, then several parties may join together and form a coalition. In this situation, the leader of the largest party is usually nominated and then elected Taoiseach.

After the new Taoiseach is presented with the seal of office from the president, he or she nominates members of the cabinet. These nominees must be approved by the Dáil. At this point, the government has been formed.

COALITION OR SINGLE PARTY GOVERNMENT?

Single party governments have traditionally been the preferred option for Fianna Fáil because of its political strength. On some of these occasions, it has held power as a minority government. 1989 was the first time FF was forced to form a coalition government to retain power.

Minority governments are those in which the government does not have a Dáil majority. It is voted into and kept in power by the votes of other political parties or independents. Unlike a coalition, these other TDs are not members of the government.

A **coalition**, sometimes called partnership government, is a government of more than one political party. This occurs because no single party has achieved an over-all majority in the Dáil. This situation is very common elsewhere in Europe because of the way the proportional representation voting system works. It has become common in Ireland. The Taoiseach is usually the leader of the largest party.

National government is a government of all the political parties. It is sometimes formed during periods of war or political unrest.

COMPOSITION OF IRISH GOVERNMENTS, 1922-1995

Dates	Major Political Parties	Taoiseach
1922-1922	Pro-Treaty/Cumann na nGaedheal	Michael Collins •
1922-1932	Cumann na nGaedheal	William Cosgrave •
1932-1948	Fianna Fáil	Éamon de Valera •
1948-1951	Fine Gael, Labour, Clann na Poblachta, National Labour, Clann na Talmhan	John A. Costello
1951-1954	Fianna Fáil	Éamon de Valera
1954-1957	Fine Gael, Labour, Clann na Talmhan	John A. Costello
1957-1973	Fianna Fáil	Éamon de Valera, Seán Lemass, Jack Lynch★
1973-1977	Fine Gael, Labour	Liam Cosgrave
1977-1981	Fianna Fáil	Jack Lynch, Charles Haughey★
1981-1982 (Feb)	Fine Gael, Labour	Garret FitzGerald
1982-1982 (Nov)	Fianna Fáil	Charles Haughey
1982-1987	Fine Gael, Labour	Garret FitzGerald
1987-1989	Fianna Fáil	Charles Haughey
1989-1992	Fianna Fáil, Progressive Democrats	Charles Haughey, Albert Reynolds★
1992-1994	Fianna Fáil, Labour	Albert Reynolds
1994-	Fine Gael, Labour, Democratic Left	John Bruton‡

• under the 1922 Constitution the position was called 'President of the Executive Council' and it was changed to Taoiseach in the 1937 Constitution.
★ indicates changeover in leadership.
‡ indicates changeover in government without an election.

GOVERNMENT IN CRISIS

Mr Harry Whelehan (left) is appointed President of the High Court.

Following the November 1992 general election, a 'partnership government' of Fianna Fáil and Labour was formed. During the summer of 1994, Taoiseach Albert Reynolds (FF) sought approval for the appointment of the attorney general, Harry Whelehan, to the post of president of the High Court. This was strongly opposed by Tánaiste Dick Spring (Lab).

About the same time, UTV broadcast a programme about Fr Brendan Smyth, who was wanted in Northern Ireland for child sexual abuse (paedophilia). It claimed that a request for his extradition had been delayed for seven months by the Irish attorney general's office. Was the delay due to incompetence or inefficiency, or was it intentional? In either case, this revelation was seen by politicians and the

media to support Spring's claim that Whelehan was unsuitable for appointment as president of the High Court.

Mr Reynolds, however, insisted on making the appointment in early November 1994. The Labour Party ministers refused to support the nomination at cabinet and walked out of that meeting. These actions precipitated a six-week government crisis.

The Dáil met to consider the appointment of Mr Whelehan to the High Court several days later. The Taoiseach explained why he acted as he did. A truce appeared likely until Mr Spring learned that the Taoiseach and several Fianna Fáil ministers had misled the Dáil about the handling of the extradition warrant. It concerned the extradition of an Irish monk to Northern Ireland for paedophilia two years earlier. This information undermined the reason given by Whelehan for the seven-month delay. Reynolds took the blame and resigned the following day as Taoiseach.

Would an election be called? Usually when a Taoiseach resigns, he or she requests the President to dissolve the Dáil and call a general election. Reynolds decided not to do this because he believed Fianna Fáil would do very badly in an election. Fianna Fáil elected a new leader within days. Over the next two weeks, Bertie Ahern (FF) negotiated a new government arrangement with Labour.

On the eve of this government being confirmed by the Dáil, new revelations about the Whelehan affair were published by *The Irish Times*. It claimed that Fianna Fáil ministers, prior to the Reynolds' speech to the Dáil, had appealed to Harry Whelehan not to pursue his swearing-in as president of the High court. If true, it meant that all Fianna Fáil ministers had known of the significance of the earlier case and had together attempted to hide this information from the Dáil. By seeking to cancel or postpone Whelehan's appointment to the High Court, they were also alleged to have interfered in the separation of powers between the executive and the judiciary.

For a second time in a month, a Fianna Fáil/Labour Party government collapsed. Again, the President was not requested to dissolve the Dáil. Negotiations began among all non-Fianna Fáil parties: Fine Gael, Labour, Progressive Democrats and Democratic Left. On 15 December, a new government was formed between Fine Gael, Labour and Democratic Left with John Bruton (FG) as Taoiseach. This was the first government formed without a general election since the formation of the state.

Accusation and counter-accusation continued for weeks. A Dáil inquiry was organised to establish the reason for the seven-month delay in processing the Brendan Smyth extradition warrants, and to investigate the claims that Fianna Fáil misled the Dáil. A report was published in February 1995.

A DAY IN THE LIFE OF THE DÁIL

The Dáil sits regularly three or four days a week, beginning on Tuesday. The order of business is discussed each day. This sets out the government's agenda: which legislation will be discussed, what issues will be debated, what questions will be answered. This is the time when the most heated exchanges between the government and the opposition occur. The opposition will usually attempt to raise issues which it feels might embarrass the government.

The parliamentary system insists that the people are sovereign. This means that the government is answerable to the Dáil, and must attend and answer questions in the

Dáil. This is why at the beginning of business each day, the cabinet is always seen walking into the Dáil chamber as a group even if individual members may leave shortly thereafter to attend to other business.

Most Dáil business takes place in the Dáil chamber. There are a number of select or special committees which discuss details of legislation or issues of policy. The number of these has increased in recent years, greatly enhancing the Dáil's role.

The government always strives to maintain a majority of TDs in the Dáil. This majority enables the government to control the Dáil agenda, and to dominate all Dáil business and all policy-making. It ensures that the government's proposals and bills are always passed.

Question Time is held every day the Dáil is in session, with minor exceptions. It provides an opportunity for TDs to question the Taoiseach and individual ministers about their policies and legislation. There is some opportunity for emergency questions to arise but generally the questions have to be submitted, in writing, at least three days in advance. There is no Question Time in the Seanad.

Seanad business is organised in a similar manner to the Dáil but it meets less frequently than the Dáil. Government ministers attend the Seanad only to discuss particular pieces of legislation. There is often a more relaxed atmosphere in the Seanad and this contributes to a more lively exchange of ideas.

Dáil business is chaired by the Ceann Comhairle. An election for this position is held on the first sitting day of the Dáil following a general election. Given the need

for the Ceann Comhairle to be seen as politically impartial, he or she is automatically returned at the next election. The Seanad is chaired by the Cathaoirleach.

THE OPPOSITION

The opposition is comprised of all non-government TDs. The largest non-government party is granted the most authority. Its leader is known as the Leader of the Opposition.

The opposition's role is to:

*   closely question the Taoiseach and members of the cabinet
*   raise and highlight issues that they feel the government has ignored
*   propose alternative legislation
*   oppose and seek to defeat the government's proposals and legislation
*   be prepared to form a government if requested to do so by the president.

THE WHIP

Being a member of a political party carries both privileges and duties. This is especially true for TDs and senators.

United, tightly disciplined political parties make certain that party members always vote with the party. If a member of a party decides not to do so, then the whip may be removed from that person.

The whip is a nonexistent item but it conjures up the idea of commanding obedience. The removal of the whip is equivalent to disciplinary action, which may involve the loss of a party office and secretary, access to research facilities, permission to attend parliamentary party meetings, etc. Party discipline also operates within the opposition parties.

IN NEED OF REFORM?

In reality, the Oireachtas plays a small role in the law-making process. Professor Basil Chubb has said that the Oireachtas does not govern, it declares laws. Power is exclusive to government.

Commentators and politicians have criticised the weakness of the Dáil for some time. These criticisms fall under four main headings:

- There are too many restrictions on what questions can be asked and what issues debated. In turn, the government cannot be compelled to answer any question fully.
- The Dáil does not sit for enough days during the year. In a normal year, the Dáil sits approximately 80 days while the Seanad sits for less than half that number. This means that many major decisions are made and issues arise when the Dáil is not in a position to discuss or question them.
- Inadequate research facilities means that TDs have to rely too heavily on the government for information.

- Unlike the American Congress, the Oireachtas has no investigative functions. It cannot hold hearings on controversial issues or investigate alleged wrong-doing.

While many TDs share these views, it suits the government that the Dáil is not in a strong position to challenge its authority. Reforms to enhance the power of the Dáil are pending.

In recent years, the Seanad has also come under increasing criticism.

- Its powers are seen as too limited and it sits too infrequently.
- The Seanad is often used by politicians seeking election to, or retirement from, the Dáil.
- The voting system is restricted to politicians and university graduates. Graduates from other newer third-level institutions are not entitled to vote for the 'university' panels.
- The fact that the Taoiseach has eleven nominees ensures that the government's point of view always dominates.

For all these reasons, some critics argue that the Seanad should be abolished. Others argue that the presence of the Seanad ensures that the power of the Dáil is balanced, a key ingredient of the principle of liberal democratic government discussed in this chapter.

Seanad Éireann is as irrelevant to Irish life today as it was when it first came into existence 40 years ago. The Senate has turned out to be all about time, technicality and tiresome trivia; [it] has become the playground of party politics ...

Geraldine Kennedy,
The Irish Times, 26 April 1978

The Senate should be abolished.

Michael McDowell, Progressive Democrats,
The Irish Times, 6 October 1987

The arguments for a second chamber are very compelling. It would be a diminution in our democratic control if we decided that because the Senate did not stand up to a critical examination we should abolish it. The Senate could play a major role in Irish life. All that's needed, is the political will.

Mary Robinson,
Senator, *The Irish Times*,
26 April 1978

ASSIGNMENTS

1   Can you list the dates when Ireland had:
    (a) a single party government?
    (b) a minority government?
    (c) a coalition government?
2   What is the difference between the 'government party' and 'the government'?
3   If the government is answerable to the Dáil, to whom is the Dáil answerable?
4   What do you think is the role of the opposition?
5   What do you think Professor Basil Chubb means when he says 'the Oireachtas does not govern, it declares laws'?
6   Why do you think it suits the government that the Dáil is not in a strong position to challenge its authority?

RESEARCH ACTIVITIES

1   Look back at the chart showing the composition of Irish governments between 1922 and 1995 on page 85. Can you find the name of the Tánaiste for each of the governments?
2   What are the names of the Dáil special and select committees?
    What do these committees do?

ACTIVITY

Organise a classroom debate: That the Seanad should be abolished.

LOCAL
GOVERNMENT

WHAT IS LOCAL GOVERNMENT?

When you use a library, a public swimming pool or park, call an ambulance or fire brigade, have your refuse collected or drink water from a tap, you are using amenities and services which have been provided by a local authority.

It is no longer practical to provide and manage this broad range of services from one central location because society has become so complex. Decision-making at central government level is no longer sufficient to meet all our needs. People want a greater say in their own affairs and those of their neighbourhood.

In most modern societies, a system of regional or local government has developed.

In Ireland we have a two-tier system. National government is one tier and local government or local authorities are the other. You know most of these local authorities as corporations, county councils, urban district councils or town commissioners.

Local government is government at local level. Local authorities have three functions:

- to administer services to the community
- to voice the opinions, needs and aspirations of the local community
- to ensure government is within reach of, and accountable to, the people.

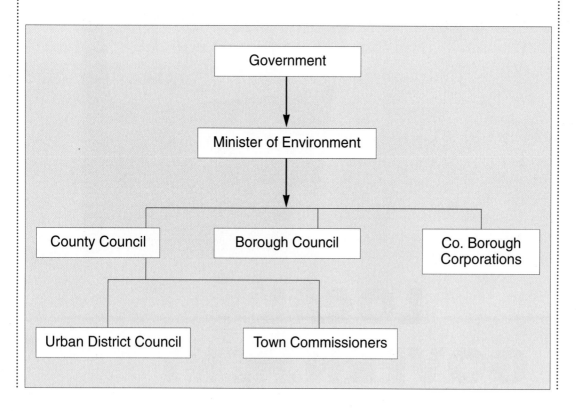

Irish local authorities are given powers and functions under legislation passed by the Oireachtas. They do not have constitutional guarantees to act independently. They have no power to raise their own taxes; most of the money they receive is from the central or national exchequer. Local authorities may only pass by-laws which carry a very minor fine, for example for illegal parking or failure to comply with building regulations.

The Minister for the Environment exercises firm control over all the activities and spending of local authorities. For example, local authorities may not hire additional staff over a quota set by the Department of the Environment. This may result in a swimming pool or library closing down at holiday times owing to staff shortages. Various other government departments also oversee the activities of local authorities.

The structure of national and local government, as shown in the diagram on page 92, is very different from what pertains in either the USA, Germany or India. These countries have a federal system. Under that system, the country is sub-divided into individual states. These states have their own constitutions, legislative structure, and legal systems. They are allowed to pass laws, and raise revenue through taxation. Each state also elects representatives to the national parliament. This situation allows the states to be relatively independent of the national government. The name of the country often illustrates its particular type of government: the Federal Republic of Germany or the United States of America.

STRUCTURE OF LOCAL AUTHORITIES

Ireland has five different categories of local authority. The basic unit is the county council, and the smallest is the board of town commissioners. Each community of more than 1,500 people can petition the Minister for the Environment for the right to be designated a town for the purposes of electing town commissioners. Large urban areas are designated county borough corporations and borough corporations, more commonly known as corporations. Urban district councils (UDC) and borough councils are local authorities for smaller urban areas. Rural district councils were abolished in 1925.

The number of elected seats on each local authority is set by law. This number varies according to the type of local authority. County councils and county borough corporations have the largest number of members, and boards of town commissioners have the smallest.

The different local authorities are:
- county councils – **29**
- county borough corporations – **5**
- borough councils – **5**
- urban district councils (UDC) – **49**
- town commissioners – **30**

The following map of County Galway shows the territorial jurisdiction of the Galway County Borough Corporation, Galway County Council, Urban District Council and town commissioners.

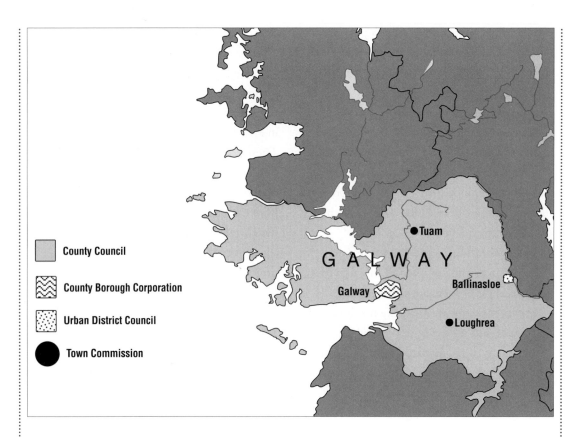

County Council

County Borough Corporation

Urban District Council

Town Commission

GALWAY

Tuam

Galway

Ballinasloe

Loughrea

The most significant change in local government structures occurred in the Dublin area in 1993. By the 1980s over one million people, one third of the total population, lived in the greater Dublin area. Many of these people officially lived in the county but worked or shopped in the city, and used roads, public transport and public amenities which crossed city and suburban boundaries. In addition, areas like Tallaght, with a population equivalent to Limerick, had no local authority.

In 1993, Dublin county was divided into three new councils: Dún Laoghaire/ Rathdown, Fingal and Dublin South councils. A new Dublin Regional Authority was created. It has representatives from these three councils plus Dublin Corporation.

ÚDARÁS NA GAELTACHTA

Údarás na Gaeltachta was established under legislation in 1979 as a local authority specifically for the Gaeltacht. It is an elected body, with three constituencies: Leinster/Ulster: 3 seats; Munster: 2 seats; Connacht: 2 seats.

It has responsibility for the linguistic, cultural, social, physical and economic development of the Gaeltacht and falls under the jurisdiction of the Minister for Arts, Culture and the Gaeltacht. The Údarás is not a local authority under the terms of the local government legislation.

FUNCTIONS AND POWERS OF LOCAL AUTHORITIES

County councils and county borough corporations have the maximum number of responsibilities of all Irish local authorities. Since 1976 these functions have been classified into eight programme groups. In contrast, town commissioners have responsibility only for the maintenance of houses, allotments, meals for school children, parks, licensing cinemas and markets, etc.

EIGHT PROGRAMME GROUPS

1. Housing and building
- management and provision of local authority housing
- assistance to persons housing themselves or improving their houses
- itinerant rehabilitation
- enforcement of certain housing standards and controls, etc.

2. Road transport and safety
- road upkeep and improvement
- public lighting
- traffic management facilities
- safety education and information
- collection of motor taxation
- licensing of draws, etc.

3. Water supply and sewage
- public water supply and sewage schemes
- assistance towards the provision of piped water supply to existing dwellings
- sewage facilities for same
- public toilets, etc.

4. Development incentives and controls
- physical planning policy
- control of new development and building
- promotion of industrial and other developments, etc.

5. Environmental protection
- waste collection and disposal
- burial grounds
- safety of structures and spaces
- fire protection
- pollution control, etc.

6. Recreation and amenity
- swimming pools
- libraries
- parks
- open spaces
- recreation centres
- art galleries
- museums
- theatres
- conservation
- improvement of all of the above.

7. Agriculture, education, health and welfare
- appointment/election of public representatives to county committees of agriculture, vocational education committees, regional health boards, regional tourism organisations, fisheries boards, harbour authorities
- joint drainage committees
- unemployment assistance
- public assistance
- rates/service charge waiver schemes.

8. Miscellaneous services
- financial management
- rates/service charge collection
- elections
- courthouses
- coroners and inquests
- consumer protection measures
- markets, fairs and abattoirs
- gas works.

ASSIGNMENTS

1 What are the different kinds of local authorities? List them in order of size.

2 Can you describe the main functions of local authorities?

3 To which programme group do the following activities belong?

   (a) road cleaning

   (b) restoration of an old building

   (c) rubbish collection

   (d) planning permission for extension to a private house

   (e) licensing for a public concert

   (f) management of graveyards

   (g) unemployment offices

   (h) vocational educational committees

   (i) making a dangerous building safe

4 Why was Dublin County Council divided into three areas in 1993?

5 Give an example of how local government should fulfil each of these objectives:

   (a) to voice the opinions, needs and aspirations of the local community

   (b) to ensure government is within reach of, and accountable to, the people

   (c) to administer services to the community.

6 Údarás na Gaeltachta is a regional authority for the Gaeltacht areas. Should it be given more powers?

RESEARCH ACTIVITIES

1 List the recreational amenities that are funded by your local authority.

2 Find out what the following committees do:

   (a) county committees of agriculture

   (b) vocational education committees

   (c) regional health boards

   (d) fisheries boards

   (e) harbour authorities

   (f) county enterprise boards.

ACTIVITIES

1 Ask your local authority for a copy of its current budget. Produce a bar chart indicating the amount of money spent on each of the different programme groups. Which areas receive the most funding? the least funding? Do you agree with how the money is spent?

2 Organise a classroom discussion: What do you think the purpose of local government should be?

HOW LOCAL GOVERNMENT WORKS

reserved functions:

the powers of the elected councillors

executive responsibility:

the administrative powers of the city and county manager

In the first decades of the twentieth century, members of local authorities were part-time and voluntary. There were few full-time staff, and councillors attempted to run the city or town after their day job. The minister had supreme authority. He could decide to abolish a local authority if he disagreed with the councillors or felt they were not doing their job properly.

Between 1929 and 1940, a new system was introduced throughout Ireland. This was known as the city and county managerial system. This system provides for a full-time manager for county councils and corporations, and elected councillors.

The **manager** is concerned with the day-to-day running of the local authority. The county manager is the chief executive for all the local authorities within the county. He or she is appointed to office by open, public competition held by the Local Appointments Board.

The manager has **executive responsibility** for:

- employing staff
- accepting tenders
- managing local authority housing
- collecting rates and rents
- day-to-day administration of the local authority.

The **councillors** are elected public representatives. Those tasks which are not specifically described as the executive functions of the manager are reserved for elected councillors. Councillors decide policy while the manager implements it. Neither the manager nor the councillors can make decisions without the approval of the other.

Councillors carry out the following **reserved functions**:

- determining policy and principle
- striking the rate
- borrowing money
- making development plans
- making, amending or revoking by-laws
- bringing enactments into force
- nominating persons to act on other public bodies.

Councillors are paid only a nominal travel allowance to cover their costs for attending meetings. With some exceptions, councillors need to work in other jobs. Doing shift-work or working irregular hours may mean that some people have difficulty participating in local government. Serving gardaí and members of the armed forces are excluded by law from contesting elections.

Local elections are held every five years, although the Minister for the Environment has the power to determine the timing of these elections. All residents of the state over eighteen years are eligible to vote. The candidate who is the first person to be elected in a Corporation local election constituency is given the title of Alderman or Alderwoman.

Each local authority usually holds monthly meetings. In addition, the large local authorities have a range of different committees which meet at least once during the month. These committees usually have their own chairperson. Membership and chairpersonship of committees is usually arranged according to the strength of the major political parties. Members of the public and the press are allowed to attend the monthly and some committee meetings.

Sometimes alliances between different political parties dominate the councils. The Civic Alliance was formed in Dublin City Council by Fine Gael, Labour Party, Workers' Party, Green Party and five community councillors in 1991 to prevent Fianna Fáil gaining control of any of the committees.

ASSIGNMENTS

1   What is the name of the system which determines the responsibilities of the manager and the councillors in Irish local government?

2   Which member(s) of the local authority has executive functions? reserved functions? What is the difference between executive functions and reserved functions?

3   How often are local government elections held?

4   Some groups of people are excluded from participating in local government. Who are they? Why are those people excluded?

ACTIVITIES

1   In which local authority area do you live? How many members does your local authority have?

2   Attend a meeting of your local council. Write a report of the meeting. Compare your report with newspaper reports of the same meeting.

3   Draw a diagram of the structure of your local authority. Who is the city or county manager? Are there any assistant managers? How many councillors are there? Are there any standing committees?

MANAGERS AND COUNCILLORS

Managers and councillors are often in conflict with each other.

The conflict of interest which local representatives face … when forced to choose between implementing new government policies … [to house] the travelling community and their own political survival placed many of them in an invidious position. The role of the elected public representative can be a difficult one in instances where the survival of the species is very definitely dependent on satisfying the will of the majority.

Cllr Michael O'Brien, reported in *The Kilkenny People*, August 1994

Councillors sometimes feel that the manager has too much power. The manager's full-time position means that he or she has a greater knowledge of local affairs and forthcoming issues. Councillors feel that this allows the manager to organise or manipulate information to support his or her particular viewpoint.

Managers often see councillors as proposing unworkable solutions or passing motions in order to grab the headlines.

To achieve a balance between councillors and the manager, legislation was introduced in 1955. This gave councillors the power to:

- demand that the manager pursue a particular action

- prevent the manager from pursuing a particular action.

THE LORD MAYOR

The lord mayor is the first citizen of the city. Election for lord mayor is an annual event, and is usually the choice of the majority party or political alliance on the local authority. The position rotates among its members and is considered a prize. In addition to chairing meetings of the council, the position is primarily ceremonial. According to protocol, the formal introduction of the lord mayor at any public gathering takes precedence over that of the Taoiseach if both are attending the same function. The president of Ireland is the only person who has priority over both the lord mayor and the Taoiseach.

Lord Mayor, John Gormley

Only Cork and Dublin have the position of lord mayor. Cork's was established in 1900, the same year as Belfast's. Dublin's dates from 1665, and was the second oldest in these islands after London. The Dublin lord mayor has the option of residing in the mansion house. He or she is given a new car annually with the first registration for the year and a full-time driver. There is a ceremonial coach for very formal events.

County councils elect a chairperson or Cathaoirleach who has the same tasks as the lord mayor.

THE DUAL MANDATE

Many councillors are simultaneously members of other local authorities as well as of the Dáil or Seanad. This is called having a dual mandate. There is no constitutional restriction on the number of public offices to which someone may be elected. About 70 per cent of TDs and senators are simultaneously members of at least one local authority.

Election to a local authority is often seen as the first step on the political ladder to election to the Dáil. Local elections are a good testing ground for potential Dáil candidates. It enables them to learn how the political system works from the inside and helps them to become well known throughout the community. New political parties and aspiring individuals often contest local elections.

Once elected to the Oireachtas, most politicians choose to retain their local authority seat. Ministers and junior ministers must, however, give up their seat on taking office. Being a member of a local authority provides politicians with ongoing knowledge of the local area which they need in order to help them retain their seat in future elections.

ASSIGNMENTS
1 Why is holding the position of mayor considered to be an honour and sometimes a prize ?
2 Why do councillors and managers sometimes come into conflict with each other?
3 What is the term used when a councillor retains membership of a local authority and of the Dáil? Why do they do this? Why do you think some people object to this?
4 Write a job description for a member of your local authority.
5 Devise a list of the changes you would make in your community if you were a local representative.

RESEARCH ACTIVITIES
1 Who are your local councillors? To which political parties do they belong? Are there any independent members of the council?
2 Use your local newspapers to find out which issues your local authority has been involved with over the past several weeks or months. List them.

HOW ARE LOCAL AUTHORITIES FUNDED?

Local authorities, like all public bodies, including the government, need money to provide and improve services and facilities. Local government revenue is raised through the following sources:

- **rates** on commercial property
- rates support grant from central government
- service charges on water, rubbish collection, library use, ambulance or fire services
- grants and subsidies from the European Union for infrastructural and road development, and for environmental improvement schemes
- miscellaneous receipts from parking meters, driving licences, local authority rents, fees for certain services, etc.

Until 1977 rates were the major source of local revenue. Rates are a levy paid on the value of all land and buildings in the state. This value or valuation is not equal to the market value. In other words, the valuation is not the sum of money one would expect to receive if the property or house was sold. Instead, it is a figure based upon the use of the property or house, its location, the quality of the land, etc.

The rating system works like this: Each year, every local authority is required to draw up a budget for the forthcoming year. This includes the anticipated out-going expenditure and in-coming revenue for the year. Based upon these estimates, each local

authority strikes a rate. This means it calculates a figure which is then multiplied against the valuation of every building and property in its area.

For example:

Valuation of a property	= £10.00
The rate or multiplier	= x £25.00
What is to be paid	= £250.00

Public unhappiness with the rates system led to the abolition of domestic rates in 1977. A Supreme Court case taken by the Irish Farmers' Association (IFA) in 1984 led to the abolition of agricultural rates. Today, rates are paid only on commercial property: by businesses, shops, factories, etc. No rates are paid on schools, churches or other special institutions.

When domestic rates were abolished, the government pledged to make up the short-fall through the rates support grant. This grant has proved to be inadequate.

In 1983, local authorities were allowed to introduce charges for water and other services. In recent years, governments have promised to review the entire funding of local government.

The funding of local authorities is a political 'hot-potato'. To keep the charges low, local services have had to be cut back. Some politicians favour the introduction of a local tax, perhaps based on property. The government's proposal to extend the existing residential property tax (RPT) in 1994 was very unpopular. Many people opposed what they saw as further taxation at a time of existing high levels of income tax (PAYE).

rates:

a financial charge made on all property based upon the use of the property

ASSIGNMENTS

1   How are local authorities funded?

2   What are service charges? Why do some people oppose them?

3   If a property is valued at £12.50 and a multiplier is set at £110, what will the owner of the property have to pay in rates?

RESEARCH ACTIVITIES

1   Write to the main political parties to find out their attitude towards local authority funding.

2   Conduct a survey in your area. Ask people how they think local government should be financed: through rates, local taxes or more money from central government?

3   In some areas of the country, people have refused to pay additional money for water and other services. Has there been a controversy over the service charges in your area? Write a newspaper article on what happened. Interview some of the people involved.

4   Outline the arguments for and against service charges.

HOW DOES LOCAL GOVERNMENT AFFECT YOU?

Planning and development is one area where local authorities have a great deal of power and influence. Decisions taken by councils can affect the way a town or city will develop in the future: how much green space there will be for parks, whether roads will take priority over the needs of cyclists and pedestrians, and where housing will be located. These decisions can often be extremely controversial.

Prior to 1963, anyone seeking to build, change the use of, or demolish a building came up against few restrictions. The Local Government (Planning and Development) Act, 1963 changed all this. It required all local authorities to prepare and implement a development plan for their area. The plan, renewed every five years, gives detailed drawings of the intended development of the town, city or county over the next years. It is a very specific map, outlining the precise locations or zones where the following types of development can occur:

- road improvements
- amenity or green belt areas
- housing
- industrial
- commercial
- renovation and preservation.

Each local authority is required to place the development proposals or plan on public display. Any member of the public can submit a written objection. Each of these objections is considered by the local authority's planners and the councillors.

Planning permission is required for any building proposal. This is granted only when the proposal corresponds with the objectives of the development plan. Any proposal which does not fit in, which might damage the environment, or is not in character with the rest of the buildings may be rejected. A new housing or factory scheme may restrict public access to a park or other public amenity, or may put too much pressure on sewage facilities.

When a proposal does not receive planning permission from a local authority, several options still remain. The most common option is to make an appeal to An Bord Pleanála.

Planning issues can often cause division and conflict within a community. One case was the controversy surrounding the building of an interpretive centre at Mullaghmore, Co. Clare. Each side in the controversy claimed to be equally concerned with the preservation of the environment but disagreed on how this should be done. Those opposed to the centre claimed its location in the heartland of the Burren would have a damaging effect on the environment. Those in favour were interested in the new (business and tourist) opportunities that might arise because of the centre in the area.

COUNCILLORS AND PLANNERS IN CONFLICT

Councillors and planners often find themselves in opposition to each other over a proposed plan or a particular application for planning permission.

Councillors may or may not choose to accept the recommendations of the local authority's planning and development section. Councillors, as democratically elected representatives, may feel that the professional planners are not acting in the interest of the public good.

Planners may feel that councillors respond too much to pressure from powerful interest and community groups in their local area and ignore the general good of the entire population.

All decisions to grant planning permission must be approved by the city or county council. The 1955 Local Government Act allows councillors to make the final decision: to approve a planning request or to prevent it going ahead.

Section 4 permits councillors to demand that the manager implement a particular decision. This has been commonly used by councillors who wish to grant planning permission in circumstances when it might go against or contravene the local authority's development plan.

Section 5 permits councillors to demand that the manager stops doing a particular action. This has often been used to prevent the demolition of an historical building.

The role of councillors has become controversial because :

- Some councillors have repeatedly used Section 4 motions to grant planning permission to build houses in scenic areas of the country. Professional planners often oppose such development because they feel it undermines the countryside. An Taisce, the National Heritage Society, reported that Donegal, Galway, Louth and Mayo county councils were the most frequent users of Section 4 motions (February 1991).
- Some councillors have supported fundamental changes in their local authority's development plans because of heavy lobbying or political pressure. One of the most common and controversial changes

to a development plan is to change land from green belt or agricultural use to housing or commercial use. Permission to **rezone** such land may substantially increase its market value and potential profit to the owner.

The Local Government Act, 1991, has tightened up on the misuse of these motions. A Section 4 motion can only be approved if three-quarters of the councillors give their assent. A simple majority is no longer enough.

'People power' is becoming quite a phenomenon in Co. Longford according to the Longford News, with concerned citizens getting together to wage a campaign on a wide range of environmental issues, from the closure of Ballymahon dump and the destructive traffic plans for Longford town to the future of the courthouse ... Meanwhile, staff and students from Longford's biggest and best known school, St Mel's College, have formed LEAF (Longford Environmental Awareness Forum) to campaign against a highly-controversial new road which would cut through the front of the college sweeping away its entrance gates and a sizeable slice of its grand avenue of mature trees. LEAF says this 'absurd' scheme is clearly designed to facilitate traffic exiting from the new shopping centre behind the east side of Main Street and shows 'blatant disregard for the environmental and aesthetic consequences' ... Father Garvey, who is currently laying out a running track on the site, told the meeting he had first become aware of the road plan when he read about it in the Longford Leader. He believed it was being pushed 'at the request of vested interests' and said he had been 'shocked at the feeling of powerlessness coming from the elected representatives'.

Frank McDonald, *The Irish Times*,
August 22, 1994

rezone:
to change the designated use of an area or district of a town, city or county

ASSIGNMENTS

1 What is a development plan?
2 What is meant by rezoning land? How can rezoning affect the value of a piece of land?
3 What is Section 4? How is it used in planning matters?
4 What action can councillors take to stop a development or the demolition of an old house?
5 Why do councillors and planners come into conflict with each other?
6 Why do you think Fr Garvey is shocked at the feeling of powerlessness coming from the elected representatives?

RESEARCH ACTIVITIES

1 Visit your local authority planning and development department. Draw a map or write a report on the development plan, showing or describing which areas are ear-marked for:
   (a) road improvements
   (b) amenity or green belt usage
   (c) housing
   (d) industrial
   (e) commercial
   (f) renovation and preservation.
2 Look through recent issues of your local newspaper. Which planning issues have been covered recently in the newspaper?
3 Make a proposal for a cycle path for your locality or town which you can submit to your local authority or councillor.
4 Find out what the Environmental Protection Agency (EPA) does? What role might it play in planning applications?
5 What is an 'environmental impact study'?

ACTIVITIES

1 Organise a classroom discussion: What are cities for?
   (a) pedestrians or cars?
   (b) people to live in or people to work in?
   How would you ensure that the city was developed to meet your view?

2   Role Play: The Planning Game

The plot of land shown here is to be redeveloped. The local authority wish to consult with the residents to find out their views. Many people are concerned with the proposed development; they each have a different view. Organise a meeting between the different residents and the planning department to resolve this issue. How can the issue be resolved? What solution is acceptable to the greatest number of people?

Your teacher is playing the part of someone from the planning department and will chair the meeting. You can devise your own list of players (residents) based upon the people you might know in your area. A suggested list of residents is as follows:

Mr Kelly is sixty-nine and dislikes children. He is concerned that his garden will be interfered with and that the value of his house will drop. He wants the land to be landscaped with plenty of flower beds to stop children playing football. He is also opposed to seats because it only encourages young people to hang around.

Mrs Cantwell is fifty-five and would like a landscaped area with plenty of seats to encourage people to sit and get to know each other.

Mr and Mrs Brady do not really mind what happens to the land as long as they can continue to exercise their dogs in the green.

Elizabeth and **Martin** are a young married couple with three children. They do not really mind what happens as long as there is a supervised playground for their children. They want dogs to be banned from the park because they feel dogs are a danger to the children and dirty the park.

Rosemary Gill is the trainer of the girls' soccer team. She want a girls' changing room and playing pitch because the girls get laughed at and pushed around by the boys at the other pitches.

Liam Lynch is the local shop owner. He wants to develop his shop and needs extra space for car parking. If he enlarges the shop he will provide eight additional jobs and will give a once-off payment to a local community group.

Susan Corrigan, the parks manager, would like to develop the land as an adventure playground. She points out that she has not received a budget allocation from the council and so cannot develop her plans at this time.

Contact is an organisation which looks after people with a mental handicap. They need land to build a residential unit. This unit will require all the land available but they have proposed that the sports facilities would be available to the local residents.

Regal Homes wish to build ten houses on the land. They are willing to pay the local authority for the site and have offered to hand over another site in part exchange. They point out that the houses will be of a very high quality which will enhance the area.

ISSUES OF LOCAL DEMOCRACY

In recent years many commentators have asked whether Irish local government adequately meets or fulfils the needs of the community.

T.J. Barrington, the author of several studies on local government, says the Irish local government system has become too centralised and bureaucratic. By this Barrington means that there are too few local authorities for the number of people in the country. Power is held by a small number of very large authorities. Ordinary people have very little chance of really influencing how their community is run. Ireland has only 118 elected bodies each representing on average 25,000 people.

Compared with local authorities in Britain and elsewhere in Europe, Irish authorities have a restricted number of powers and a limited range of functions. Local authorities elsewhere are involved in a wider range of activities:

- public transport management and policy-making
- education management and policy-making

- police authorities
- welfare services
- health and hospital administration.

In Ireland, these services are administered primarily by the national government with very little involvement by local communities.

Proposals to allow local and regional authorities to make more decisions themselves and to restrict ministerial control or interference have regularly been discussed. Without direct control over how much money is raised, local councils have little influence on how to spend the money. It is similar to young people being restricted in what they buy because their parents are paying for it.

The Expert Advisory Committee on Local Government Reform proposed involving the community in more aspects of local decision-making. However, to give more power to local authorities and communities would necessitate taking power away from the minister and government. To date, no minister has been willing to give up such powers.

ASSIGNMENTS

1 What do you think T.J. Barrington means when he writes 'The Irish local government system has become too centralised and bureaucratic'?

2 Should ordinary citizens have a greater role in decision-making? Should local authorities involve community or sporting groups in decision-making? How do you think this could be accomplished? Write a short essay.

3 Do you think Irish authorities should become involved in a wider range of activities? Which additional services do you think should be added to the list for Irish local authorities?

POLICY-MAKING

WHAT IS A PLURALIST SOCIETY?

In the past, people's behaviour and views were strongly influenced by their family and their immediate surroundings. Most people did not travel abroad, read international newspapers and magazines or have access to television and radio. People tended to live out their lives within their community. Today, people live in a much more complex and changing world. They are likely to be introduced to many and different kinds of experiences.

People's experiences vary depending on whether they are, for example:

- in work or unemployed

- living in an urban, rural or small-town environment

- living in private, local authority or rented accommodation
- Catholic, Protestant, Jewish, Muslim or other religious belief
- male or female, white or black.

Your experiences, political views and religious values are no longer likely to be the same as your neighbour's. You may not have the same solution to the same problem. Your needs and interests may come into conflict with those of others in your community.

Societies that are made up of people with varying points of view and experiences are called **pluralist** societies. A pluralist society is one that recognises and values this diversity. A non-pluralist society is one where difference is frowned upon.

pluralist:
consisting of more than one viewpoint or belief, ethnic or religious group, etc.

1 Dublin Synagogues   2 Irish Jewish Art and Literat

DECISION-MAKING IN A DEMOCRATIC SOCIETY

consensus:

the general agreement or majority opinion

From your own experience, you know that you cannot always reach an amicable or friendly agreement with your friends or your neighbours. In other words, **consensus** or having a common view is not always possible.

In Ireland, as elsewhere, it is often difficult to reach a consensus. The government may have difficulty finding a solution that satisfies everyone. Since decision-making in a pluralist society can be a difficult process, the government must strive to:

* strike a balance between the different opinions and needs of people
* reach a consensus or a fair solution with which most people will be happy and which they will support.

Sometimes, however, consensus is not possible. Then the government must make a decision in order to:

* introduce legislation in the public good
* protect a minority against the majority
* defend the under-privileged.

The following three examples demonstrate how opinion can be sharply divided on important issues.

NUCLEAR POWER *versus* NON-NUCLEAR POWER

Many people favour nuclear power because it is an inexpensive and everlasting form of electricity. They feel that it helps industry to expand and thus create employment. Trade unions, on behalf of workers in the British nuclear fuel power stations, say that nuclear energy is safe: If it were not safe, would we be working in it?

People who oppose nuclear power claim it is dangerous to people and the environment. They want nuclear power

stations and reprocessing plants, such as Sellafield and Thorp, decommissioned or closed down. They say that radiation leaks caused by accidents do not 'respect national boundaries'. A proposal that Ireland should build a nuclear power station at Carnsore Point, Wexford, was strongly opposed in 1979. Instead of nuclear power, opponents favour the use of other energy sources: oil, gas, wind, water power, biomass and alternative fuels.

INCREASED PUBLIC SERVICES *versus* PUBLIC EXPENDITURE CUTS

To provide better and expanded public services (health care, schools, libraries, sports facilities, gardaí, museums, etc.) requires continued funding from the national exchequer. Money for these services is usually raised by taxation. The government can do this by deducting money from workers' wages (PAYE), taxing items that people buy (VAT), taxing banks and businesses (corporate tax), or taxing property and land. Taxation means less money in someone's pocket but more for the public services which benefit everyone in society.

People who favour low taxation want to cut back on the amount that the state spends. This would reduce the level of taxation but it would also lead to a reduction or loss of many services. They also say that taxation is an unnecessary interference by government in the lives of people.

A UNITED IRELAND *versus* NORTHERN IRELAND REMAINING IN UK

To establish a single state with one government for the entire island of Ireland has been a long-standing objective of Irish nationalists. Yet, a united Ireland is opposed by unionists because they consider themselves British or Ulster and wish to remain part of the United Kingdom.

RESEARCH ACTIVITY

Your experiences, political views and religious values are likely to be different from those of an elderly relation or neighbour. Devise a questionnaire to discover the differences in the lifestyle of a young person today and years ago. You can use these sample questions or devise your own.

(a)   How many children are in your family?

(b)   How many people live in your household?

(c)   At what age did you leave school?

(d)   How did you get to school?

(e)   What age were you when your family got its first car, telephone, washing machine, television, or video recorder?

(f)   What kind of household chores did you do?

(g)   Did you go on holidays? Where did you go?

(h) How often did you go to church?

(i) What did you and your friends do for fun?

(j) Did you have any friends of a different religion to yourself?

(k) At what age did you first meet someone from outside Ireland?

(l) Were any of your friends' parents separated or living apart?

(m) At what age did you receive sex education?

ACTIVITIES

1 Organise a classroom discussion concerning one of the issues on pages 111 and 112:

(a) What are the differences between the two viewpoints?

(b) Which groups of people do you think are likely to support each viewpoint?

(c) Why do you think these different viewpoints have arisen?

(d) Is a compromise or consensus between the two views possible?

(e) How would you propose reaching a consensus?

(f) In what way do you think the government should attempt to reconcile the different views?

2 Draw up a list of issues where you think consensus may not be possible. Use the questions above to examine the different viewpoints in greater detail.

PRESSURE GROUPS

In pluralist democracies, people elect representatives to speak and act on their behalf. In order to maximise their powers of persuasion, they also organise themselves into pressure groups to lobby government. These pressure groups do not wish to take over government but to influence public opinion, the media, the government and all political parties.

This is an important part of democracy. Think about what would happen if the government refused to meet with or acknowledge the wishes of the people.

There are two kinds of pressure groups in Ireland. There are those that:

(a) protect and promote the interests of its members; for example:
- Irish Farmers' Association (IFA)
- Irish Congress of Trade Unions (ICTU)
- Irish National Organisation of the Unemployed (INOU)

(b) promote a cause; for example:
- Green Peace
- Irish Council against Blood Sports
- Irish Commission for Justice and Peace
- An Taisce

113

Pressure groups work in a variety of ways. They lobby ministers, civil servants, the media and ordinary politicians in order to influence policy. They might do any or all of the following:

- write letters to their TD, or the appropriate minister
- write letters to the newspapers
- have a meeting with their TD, the appropriate minister or civil servant
- organise a petition
- organise a public campaign
- participate in a demonstration or public protest meeting
- organise a press conference to be covered on television, radio or newspapers
- organise a picket outside the Dáil, appropriate local authority or European Union offices
- run for election
- vote only for candidates who support their views.

Compared with other European countries and the USA, Ireland has fewer groups organised to promote a particular issue or cause. This is because Irish people tend to approach politicians individually to pursue change or resolve problems, rather than form or join an association. Nevertheless, people who organise themselves into groups, however small, can often make an impact on government which is disproportionate to their actual size.

In recent years several campaigns have been organised to influence legislation. Some of them have been more successful than others. These include the campaign:

- to close Sellafield and stop the Thorp nuclear power reprocessing station
- to ban live hare coursing
- to improve services for people with a mental handicap
- to retain the Shannon stop-over
- to prevent the closure of hospitals
- to introduce divorce
- to allow abortion information
- to restrict abortion information.

Many people have been willing to go to great lengths to press their point of view and influence public opinion and the government. In the early 1900s, women pursuing the right to vote chained themselves to the House of Commons' railings. During the Vietnam war, American men opposed to the war preferred to go to jail or leave the country permanently. Animal rights activists have slashed fur coats and destroyed research facilities which they claim treat animals cruelly. Irish language speakers have chosen to go to jail rather than pay a TV licence which was not in the Irish language. How far would you go?

CAMPAIGN FOR A HELICOPTER RESCUE SERVICE

In 1988, a Donegal fisherman was injured on board his fishing trawler. Although the accident happened in sight of land, there was no air-sea rescue service available on the western seaboard at that time. The air corps helicopters were based near Dublin and did not have sufficient range to carry out such operations. The fisherman bled to death on board his boat.

Angered by this, Joan McGinley, a Derry-born woman living in Donegal, called a public meeting to protest at the poor level of service. Her highly successful campaign lobbied for a radical overhaul of the air-sea rescue service. After a number of years, the government was forced to establish a rescue service based at Shannon with additional support along the western coastline.

ASSIGNMENTS

1 What is a pluralist society or democracy?
2 Why is decision-making difficult in a pluralist society?
3 How and why do people seek to influence public opinion?

RESEARCH ACTIVITIES

1 Look through newspapers. Identify those issues that have given rise to the formation of pressure groups. List the issues and the pressure groups.
2 Draw up a list of pressure groups that seek to:
   (a) protect and promote the interests of its members
   (b) promote a cause.

ACTIVITIES

1 Identify a local issue that you or your friends feel strongly about. This could be a proposal for a pedestrian crossing, a cycle-path, the development of a plot of waste land or the cleaning up of a local waterway. Invite a public representative to your school and present him or her with your proposal.
2 Organise a classroom discussion: Choose an issue and discuss how far you would go to influence public opinion and the government.
   (a) Would you sign a petition?
   (b) Would you attend a lawful demonstration?
   (c) Would you deliberately break the law?
   (d) Would you deliberately damage property?
   (e) Would you be prepared to go to jail?

WHO HAS INFLUENCE IN SOCIETY?

As Irish society becomes more complex, the number of pressure groups has grown. How does government decide which group to listen to? Is it the largest? the noisiest? the one in the minister's constituency? Should priority be given to some groups over others?

It would seem that in Ireland, the social partners, the media, directives of the EU, and the Catholic church, have a large influence in determining the type of legislation passed by government, and the framing of the annual budget.

THE SOCIAL PARTNERS

Since the 1950s in Ireland, the government has brought trades unions, employers and farming organisations together for discussions as social partners in the development of the economy. These discussions are known as

Pictured at a pre-Budget 1995 meeting between the ICMSA delegation and the Minister for Finance, Mr. Quinn, discussing the ICMSA Pre-Budget Submission were left to right: the Minister, Mr. Ruairi Quinn, Mr. Con Scully, ICMSA Deputy President and Mr. Tom O'Dwyer, ICMSA President.

tripartite arrangements. They have led to a series of agreements, covering wages and salaries, employment targets, taxation, and the provision of health, education and social services.

The discussions and agreements are usually negotiated between representatives of workers, employers, farmers and the government. However, not every one is happy with this. The National Organisation of the Unemployed (INOU) and groups representing other disadvantaged people in Irish society are unhappy that they are not included.

Another noticeable feature of these talks is that they take place entirely outside the Dáil. They are only briefly discussed by the Dáil and do not need to be passed by it to be implemented. Nevertheless, these agreements form the basis of economic policy in Ireland.

TRADES UNIONS

The trades unions are represented by the Irish Congress of Trades Unions (ICTU). Its membership is made up of sixty-six unions or 677,560 members (north and south) who elect representatives to the national executive of the ICTU. Approximately 55 per cent of all employed people are members of trades unions – one of the highest membership rates in western Europe.

EMPLOYERS

The major employers' organisation is the Irish Business and Employers' Confederation (IBEC). Formed in 1992, it is a national organisation representing 4,000 firms.

tripartite:

involving three groups or parts

FARMERS

The Irish Farmers' Association (IFA) and the Irish Creamery Milk Suppliers' Association (ICMSA) are the two main farming organisations. The IFA is the largest, with a membership of 85,000 people. The ICMSA has 45,000 members. They are included in the discussions because farming is a major industry and employer.

ASSIGNMENTS

1   Who are the social partners?
2   Which groups are excluded from the tripartite arrangements between the social partners?
3   Why do you think some groups are excluded?
4   What kind of issues are dealt with in these tripartite agreements?

RESEARCH ACTIVITIES

1   Write to the following organisations and find out what their aims are: ICTU, IBEC, INOU, IFA and ICMSA.
2   What is the name of the current agreement between the social partners? What issues are included in the agreement?

THE MEDIA

The media – television, radio and newspapers – sets the agenda of political concerns. This means that the media helps to influence the major issues of the day. The media also influences public opinion by the amount and type of coverage and analysis that it gives to these issues. This is possible because we learn about what is happening in the world each day by what we hear on the radio, see on the television or read in the newspapers.

The media helps shape public opinion. It does this by:

- determining what are the news stories of the day
- choosing and using particular photographs
- highlighting particular issues by giving them more coverage than other issues
- demoting issues by ignoring them
- exposing political scandal
- favourably covering particular politicians or parties
- providing a forum for those either favouring or opposing the government.

In some countries, the press and broadcasting services are directly controlled by the government. When this happens, the media acts as a tool or agent of the state.

The news is then presented as the official version of events or as propaganda.

During the 1930s, Adolf Hitler recognised how powerful the media could be in putting across views that were favourable to the Nazis.

Journalists … like to describe the press as a great power in the state. As a matter of fact, its importance really is immense. It cannot be overestimated, for the press really continues education into adulthood.

Its readers, by and large, can be divided into three groups: first, into those who believe everything they read; second, into those who have ceased to believe anything; third, into the minds which critically examine what they read, and judge accordingly.

Numerically, the first group is by far the largest. It consists of the great mass of the people and consequently represents the simplest-minded part of the nation.

Adolf Hitler, *Mein Kampf*, 1924

In a democratic society, the media is usually viewed as the most important source of information. It helps people make informed choices about issues and government. When the media acts like this, it is called a 'watchdog'. To make sure that the media does not become a powerful tool in the hands of powerful people, some states have introduced regulations.

These regulations may restrict the number of newspapers, television, radio or satellite stations that may be owned by one company or an individual. They also protect individuals against false accusations, such as libel and defamation. Irish legislation prohibits anything or anyone being seen or heard on television or radio which may promote or incite crime, or endanger the security of the state. Sections 18 and 31 of the Broadcasting Act are used for this purpose. Censorship legislation prohibits the publication or broadcasting of anything which may be considered indecent or obscene.

RTE was prohibited from interviewing Gerry Adams, president of Sinn Féin, under Section 31 of the Broadcasting Act until 1994.

RTE is a public broadcasting station. According to law, it must give fair and balanced coverage to all points of view in its programming and in debates. Neither its journalists nor its programmes can favour a particular point of view. To make sure balance is maintained at election time, RTE apportions air time to political parties according to their electoral strength.

In contrast, the newspapers and commercial radio are privately owned. When a single individual or company owns a large percentage of the media in any country, it can pose a threat to democracy. The owner may choose to give favourable or unfavourable coverage to any issue, politician, political party or organisation. In this way, the media can be very powerful.

ASSIGNMENTS

1 How do you think the media sets the political agenda?
2 What do you think the effect would be if the government controlled the news?
3 Do you think a free and critical press is important in a democracy?
4 Which world events have affected or moved you because of the way that they were presented on television?
5 Look up the words 'libel' and 'defamation' in your dictionary. Write a definition in your own words.

ACTIVITIES

1 Look at the morning or evening papers of a single day.
   (a) What is the major story in each paper?
   (b) How many papers carry the same story?
   (c) Why was this issue chosen to be the major story?
   (d) Have photographs been used?
   (e) What are the photographs saying about the story or the people involved?
   (f) How similar or dissimilar is the newspaper coverage of the story?
   (g) Does a particular point of view come across in the way the story is told?
2 Do the following exercise with the television news from RTE, and from either BBC, ITV or SKY:
   (a) Describe the visuals that are shown. Why do you think they were chosen to illustrate the story?
   (b) Do the Irish and British stations choose to highlight different news stories?
   (c) Do the Irish and British stations tell the same stories in similar or dissimilar ways?
   (d) In what way does the news story differ?

3 Do the following exercise with radio news from RTE, and from your local station(s).

   (a) How does radio, using neither visuals nor photographs, tell the story?

   (b) Do RTE and the local station choose to highlight different news stories?

   (c) Do RTE and the local station tell the same stories in similar or dissimilar ways?

   (d) In what way does the news story differ?

4 Organise a classroom debate:

   (a) That laws should prohibit individuals from being seen or heard on television or radio if they are likely to promote or incite crime, or endanger the security of society.

   (b) That laws should prohibit the publication or broadcasting of anything which may be considered indecent or obscene.

THE EUROPEAN UNION

Ireland joined the European Community in 1973. Since then, the Single European Act (1986) and the Maastricht Treaty (1992) have increased the influence of European decisions over wide areas of Irish life. Three amendments to the constitution (1973, 1986, 1992) have been passed to permit decisions of the European Commission, the European Parliament or the European Court to take precedence over Irish law. (See chapter 9 for a full discussion.)

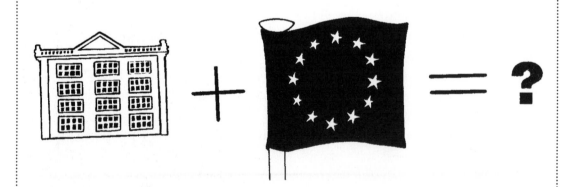

THE CATHOLIC CHURCH

The Catholic Church is one of the most powerful pressure groups in Ireland. Since the founding of the state, legislation and public policy have been strongly influenced by Catholic moral and ethical values.

Some of the most notable examples of this influence are found in the following:

- Censorship of Film Act, 1922
- Censorship of Publications Act, 1929
- Health Bill, 1951 (Mother and Child Scheme controversy)
- Health (Family Planning) Act, 1979
- Bunreacht na hÉireann, 1937
- the 8th Amendment, 1984 (Art. 40.3.3).

In 1930, a different kind of controversy arose over the appointment of Letitia Dunbar-Harrison as the County Mayo Librarian. She was a Protestant graduate of Trinity College. The Mayo Library Board refused her appointment on the grounds that her background was unsuitable for supervising reading material for a mainly Catholic community. The issue was raised in the Dáil in June 1931. Éamon de Valera supported the board's rejection of the appointment, saying that similar criterion would apply if a Protestant doctor was appointed in a Catholic area. In the end, Ms Dunbar-Harrison was given a different job.

In recent years, there have been other issues: government proposals for family planning, sex education in schools, abortion information, divorce and the ownership of schools. These events indicate the difficult and complicated issues that arise for lawmakers when the overwhelming majority of the population is of a single religion.

We have repeatedly declared that we in no way seek to have the moral teaching of the Catholic Church become the criterion of constitutional change or to have the principles of Catholic faith enshrined in civil law. What we have claimed, and must claim, is the right to fulfil our pastoral duty; and our pastoral duty is to alert the consciences of Catholics to the moral consequences of any proposed piece of legislation and to the impact of that legislation on the moral quality of life in society; while leaving to the legislators and to the electorate their freedom to act in accordance with their consciences.

Cardinal Cathal Daly, 1984

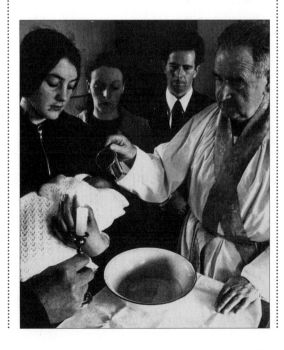

LEGISLATION

The first step in making legislation begins with the idea. Which laws should be introduced? Should a particular law be amended, updated or replaced?

Most political parties seek election on the basis of the policies which the party stands for. These policies are usually discussed at its party conference. Then they are presented in the party's election manifesto. A party's performance in government will be judged on how well it implements its proposals.

Once a government is formed, the various members of the cabinet will be requested to bring forth legislation in line with the programme for government. Each minister will probably first choose to consult with a wide range of groups about each proposal. These groups will represent people most likely to be affected by the new legislation. They will tell the minister what they think should be done.

Government must then weigh up the different opinions. Which views will it take on board and which ones will it ignore? On economic issues, it will consult the social partners and try to work out a consensus. It will need to conform to the directives and regulations of the European Union.

The government may be able to ignore the media if the public is convinced that the proposal is a good one.

If the issue involves a moral question, the government will probably consult the Catholic hierarchy. Representatives of the other churches may also be consulted. The government may employ a public relations agency to help it get its point across.

After this wide-ranging series of talks, a bill will begin to take shape. It will be discussed at cabinet, and possibly with other members of the party in the Oireachtas, known as the parliamentary party. The Department of Finance will be consulted because most legislation will cost something to implement. The attorney general will consider whether there are any constitutional or legal difficulties. Finally the bill will be written up in legal language.

The bill must be passed by both the Dáil and the Seanad. There are five steps or readings that a bill must go through in order to become a law:

- 1st Reading: introduction of the bill
- 2nd Reading: basic principles of the bill discussed
- 3rd Reading or Committee Stage: detailed discussion of the bill, when amendments may be made
- 4th Reading or Report Stage: discussion of amended bill and additional amendments may be made
- 5th Reading or Final Stage: final vote on the amended bill.

When the bill has passed all stages in one chamber, it is then discussed in the other chamber. The Dáil may reject a bill at any time but the Seanad may only amend it.

When the bill has been passed by both the Dáil and the Seanad, it goes to the president. The president must sign all bills into law. If, for any reason, the president has

constitutionality: *a law or policy decision being in accordance with the constitution*

doubts about its **constitutionality**, the council of state may be convened to give advice. The president can then decide to:

- sign the bill into law
- send the bill to the Supreme Court to consider whether it is constitutional.

Once a bill becomes law it is called an Act. It is the job of the minister and the civil service to implement it.

THE BUDGET

The budget is announced with a fan-fare of publicity by the Minister for Finance who is generally photographed carrying a briefcase. The budget, however, is one of four stages in organising the country's finances each year:

- **Estimates of Public Services:** outlines in which areas the government intends to spend money in the coming year
- **White Paper of Receipts and Expenditures:** shows how much the government has collected in taxes and other receipts in the previous year and anticipated earnings in coming year
- **Budget:** says how the government intends to raise money to fund these activities
- **Finance Bill:** puts into law the changes, usually concerning taxation, necessary to raise the needed money.

The budget is presented to the Dáil every winter, usually in February. By law, the Finance Bill must be presented to the Dáil by 30 April each year.

POLITICAL CLOUT

Democracies work on the principle that all people are equal. Each person's vote has the same value as the next person's. Does this equality extend to making laws? Do some groups in society have more influence than others?

People from lower-income groups often complain that they do not have the same political clout or influence as people from upper income or professional classes. They are less likely to have access to telephones, photocopiers or fax machines – all of which contribute to helping get a message across and gaining public support. They may find it difficult to raise money for their campaign. In contrast, those individuals or groups which are well funded and organised are more likely to be listened to and have their demands met.

Government may consider some groups to be more important than others. This might be because:

- they represent a large group of people in the country or in a particular area
- they are very well organised
- they are well funded
- they are major employers
- they own significant wealth
- the government needs to boost its support among the public or a section of the population.

Sometimes a campaign may benefit from a government or political party's determination, in difficult circumstances, to hold on to power or win seats in an election. One example is the successful campaign to insert an amendment protecting the right to life of the unborn into the constitution (Article 40.3.3).

Between 1981-82, there were three general elections in quick succession creating a period of political instability. In the run-up to the November 1982 election, both Garret FitzGerald (leader of Fine Gael) and Charles Haughey (leader of Fianna Fáil) were anxious to increase their party's share of the vote. They both publicly supported the proposed wording from the Society for the Protection of the Unborn (SPUC) for a constitutional amendment protecting the 'life of the unborn'.

After the election, a new Fine Gael/ Labour government was formed. The promised referendum was held in September 1983 using the SPUC wording. After a very acrimonious campaign, the amendment was carried (Article 40.3.3).

Another example is the influence that Ulster unionists can sometimes have on the British government. In recent years, the British prime minister has had to rely on unionists to support him in crucial votes in the House of Commons.

Do these examples represent a minority manipulating a political situation in order to exert its influence? Or does this represent democracy at its best?

ACTIVITIES

1   Organise a classroom discussion: How do we safeguard democracy against people or groups abusing their power? their wealth?

2   Collect information about environmentalist and feminist organisations.
    What does each group stand for? What impact, if any, have these organisations had on Irish politics?

POLITICAL PARTIES
AND POLITICIANS

WHAT ARE POLITICAL PARTIES?

In modern democratic societies, political parties occupy centre stage in the political process. Whether in the Oireachtas, on television or radio, in newspapers or at election time, political parties help shape our knowledge and understanding of society, and of the world around us. They help to set the **political agenda**.

People elect politicians to represent their interests and reflect their views. In turn, politicians are members of political parties which compete with each other for popular support according to different political philosophies and policies. Political parties aim to win government office – the seat of political power – in order to implement their policies.

The key aspirations of a political party are:

• to influence and shape national decision-making, ideals and values
• to seek popular support
• to build a permanent organisation
• to win elections and political power.

Political parties play an essential role in democratic politics by:

• encouraging people's participation in the political system
• channelling members' and supporters' views to the government.

Some people think that these tasks are so important that political parties should receive public funds to help them.

The right to form associations and unions, such as political parties and other associations, is recognised in Article 40.6.1.iii of *Bunreacht na hÉireann*. This is an important protection against any government which might want to restrict or prohibit the opinions or activities of political opponents.

Societies which have many political parties are known as **multi-party states**. Some countries, such as Saudi Arabia, Kuwait and Jordan, have a **no-party** system because the ruling family has prohibited the formation of political parties. China, North Korea and Cuba are examples of **one-party states**, with power held by the communist party.

Political parties must be registered in order to be included on the ballot paper after a candidate's name. There are eleven registered parties in Ireland. Not all of these have members elected at either national or local government level. There are also parties which are not registered.

political agenda: *when issues are topical or in the news, they are said to be on the political agenda*

Political parties registered to contest all elections (as of January 1995):

Fianna Fáil

Fianna Gael

The Labour Party

Progressive Democrats

Democratic Left

The Green Party/Comhaontas Glas

The Workers' Party

Sinn Féin

Comhar Críostaí

   − The Christian Solidarity Party

The Communist Party of Ireland

The Natural Law Party

ASSIGNMENTS

1   Describe the functions and activities of a political party.

2   Do you think that political parties are a necessary part of public life today?

3   In what way do political parties attempt to influence public opinion?

4   Would you join a political party? Why or why not?

RESEARCH ACTIVITIES

1   Find out which party or parties presently form the government.

2   List the political parties represented in the Dáil. How many members do they have each?

3   Who are the leaders of the political parties represented in the Dáil?

4   Which other countries have multi-party, no-party and one-party systems? List them.

ACTIVITIES

1   Organise a classroom discussion: Do you think that a government should be able to limit or restrict the 'right' to form a political party? If so, in what circumstances?

2   Organise a classroom debate: That political parties are such an important part of democratic society that people should be required to join one.

THE ORIGIN OF POLITICAL PARTIES

The earliest political parties were formed by powerful elites representing the aristocracy and the monarchy. In parliament, they joined together to defend inherited wealth and privilege. They paid little attention to the majority of people.

The Industrial Revolution (1760s–1830s) brought about many changes. Two new social groups, the capitalists and the working class, emerged. They opposed the political and economic power of the aristocracy. They also demanded the right to vote and elect representatives to parliament. Gradually the right to vote (the suffrage) was extended to include all adults in society. As a result, large numbers of people were enfranchised.

A second generation of political parties developed. In place of the old type of party of elites, mass political parties were formed. These parties brought together people who shared common interests and beliefs, or ideology. For example, European socialist parties were formed to oppose the older conservative parties and to represent the concerns of the working class and the trade union movement.

Irish political parties have been formed for similar reasons. They comprise:

- members who have a similar livelihood
- members who share similar views on national unity
- members who favour political or economic reform
- members who have a concern for a particular issue
- members who share similar moral values.

IDEOLOGY AS A 'WORLD-VIEW'

When people describe political parties, they often refer to the party as having a particular **'ideology'** or of its members taking an ideological view. This can highlight the way different people or groups of people view or understand what is happening in the world. It is a way of referring to someone's political philosophy.

When ideology is used in this way it means: an organised set of ideas, beliefs and opinions about human society. It is a way of thinking about how society is, and how society ought to be organised.

As we grow up, we realise that people hold different points of view, particularly about what should be done to solve the many problems of society. What appears the obvious solution to you may not appear so to someone else. These different and often conflicting beliefs reflect our different experiences of life.

Our experiences are heavily influenced by:

- the experiences of our daily life
- where we live: in the city or the country
- our religion, ethnicity, race and gender
- whether family members are employed or unemployed
- the historical circumstances in which we live
- whether we live in the developed or developing world
- whether there is political strife or unrest, or peace in our country
- what is happening in the world around us.

ideology:

a set of beliefs or values about society, how it should be governed, and its future development

128

ASSIGNMENTS

1   How might the experiences of a young person on a small farm, in a public housing estate or in an affluent neighbourhood in Ireland influence his/her world-view?

2   How have your circumstances or experiences influenced your own world-view? List the key influences on your views.

LEFT VERSUS RIGHT

One way to define different ideological views is to classify them according to their position on the political spectrum. The origin of the distinction between left and right emerged from the seating arrangements of the French Assembly after the French Revolution in 1789. Those on the right were the nobility believing in tradition and privilege, and those on the left were the commoners seeking change.

Political ideas are complex and often difficult to categorise but the broad distinctions between left and right are still universally used. They distinguish between basic core values, beliefs and objectives.

The circumstances and complexity of modern life have produced a political landscape that can appear very confusing

and bewildering. The disappearance of the aristocracy and powerful monarchies, and the collapse of communism makes it often difficult to distinguish between left and right. Issues of personal morality such as homosexuality, abortion, contraception and divorce are sometimes supported by people on both the left and the right. Similarly, support for Irish unity is not divided according to left/right lines.

Yet, many of the issues and principles for which men and women fought years ago remain important today. Poverty, unemployment, inequality, discrimination, crime, the environment, and civil rights are major issues of our time. In Ireland, as elsewhere, whether people are on the left or the right indicates their views and their solutions to these issues.

People on the left believe that:

- society should benefit the common good

- people are different but everyone should be treated equally

- everyone should contribute to society through taxation

- society should help people who are less well off, sick or unemployed through social welfare (the welfare state)

- society should regulate profit and competition to make sure that everyone benefits (it should intervene in the economy).

People on the right believe that:

- society should benefit the individual

- people are different and therefore not equal

- taxation does not allow individuals to choose how to spend their own money

- people who work should be rewarded and helped

- society should not regulate profit and competition (it should allow the economy to be – **laissez–faire** – and not intervene).

laissez-faire: French for 'allow it to be', it is the belief that government should intervene as little as possible in economic affairs

ASSIGNMENTS

1   Using your dictionary, write a definition of the following terms in your own words:
   (a) equality
   (b) liberty
   (c) common good
   (d) welfare state
   (e) competition.

2   In your own words, explain what people on the right and on the left believe.

3   Do you think the right still represents the values of privilege and tradition, and the left still represents disadvantage and change?

4   Identify whether the following statements represent a view of the right or of the left:
   (a) Unemployment is caused by too many people being lazy.
   (b) Society should help people who find themselves unemployed or in poor health.
   (c) All people should be treated equally by society.
   (d) There should be a minimum wage to protect people against exploitation.
   (e) I should be able to do anything I wish with my property.
   (f) Providing health and welfare services encourages people to be lazy and dependent.
   (g) Why should I pay taxes to help provide a bus service when I drive my own car?
   (h) Education is a right, not a privilege.

5   Describe your own political beliefs.

POLITICAL IDEOLOGIES

Distinctions between left and right only tell us the broad picture. Between these two goalposts, there is a complex system of political ideas or ideologies. Again, the French Revolution is the starting point. At that time, there were three different perspectives on the events taking place.

- **Edmund Burke** criticised the events in France. He wrote *Reflections on the Revolution in France*, 1790, to defend tradition and stability against revolution and chaos.

Society requires not only that the passions of individuals should be subjected, but that even in the mass body as well as in the individuals, the inclinations of men should frequently be thwarted, their will controlled, and their passions brought into subjection. This can only be done by a power out of themselves …

- **Thomas Paine** replied in his book *The Rights of Man*, 1791, which advocated political liberty and equality.

… all agree in establishing one point, the unity of man; by which I mean, that men are all of one degree, and consequently that all men are born equal, and with equal natural right, in the same manner as if posterity had been continued by creation instead of generation …

- **Sylvain Marechal** wrote the *Manifesto of the Equals* in 1796. He believed that equality meant equality of wealth.

We declare ourselves unable any longer to tolerate a situation in which the great majority of men toil and sweat in the service and at the pleasure of a tiny minority … Let there be no differences between human beings other than those of age and sex. Since all have the same needs and the same families, there should be a common education and a common supply of food for all …

These three views formed the basis of modern political ideology. Each *-ism* presents a different perspective of the world and proposes a different solution to society's many problems:

- Conservatism (Edmund Burke)
- Liberalism (Thomas Paine)
- Socialism (Sylvain Marechal)

Over the years, the number of political ideologies has grown because of differences of opinion on some key issues. Some political parties call themselves by the name of their ideology, others do not. The following is a summary of the major political ideologies of the modern world.

Communism originated in the monastic belief that all property belonged to everyone in the community. Communism – like social democracy and democratic socialism – is based on the writings of Karl Marx. His nineteenth-century writings criticised capitalism as an economic system dominated by a small but powerful class. The Russian Revolution, led by Lenin in 1917, provided an example of a 'class-less society', where all the fruits of society were shared out according to each person's needs. These ideas influenced people around the world who fought for independence from colonialism (China, Vietnam, Zimbabwe, South Africa, Chile, Cuba and Nicaragua) and against fascism. Despite 'successes' in providing extensive health care, housing, education, and employment for all, communism collapsed in eastern Europe during the 1980s.

Social democracy is a belief that social equality can be achieved by redistributing wealth from the rich to the poor by 'reforming' capitalism. Social democracy argues that everyone must have equal access to the resources of society. It has been one of the major influences on European society since World War II. It is usually associated with support for the welfare state (provision of social and medical services to all).

LEFT

Communism

Democratic Socialism

Social Democracy

Environmentalism

Democratic socialism is the belief that inequality in society is the result of vast differences in the ownership of wealth under capitalism. Political power is dominated by those who control the economy (business, banking, etc). In order to make sure that the social and economic resources of society benefit everyone, government must challenge vested interests and introduce changes in society. Policies should favour egalitarianism, and encourage people to actively participate in decision-making.

Environmentalism is not a comprehensive political ideology. It is primarily concerned with questions of pollution, waste and the environment. Radical 'greens' are very critical of consumerism and competitive economic growth, and urge the adoption of small-scale, co-operative economic activity. Environmentalism emerged as a major political movement in the 1970s with the formation of green parties.

Centrism, sometimes called 'populism', combines beliefs from both 'left' and 'right'. It portrays itself as representing the 'people' rather than any particular social class or ideology. It tries to bring the nation together in a single mass political party or 'movement'.

Liberalism. Eighteenth-century liberals strongly believed in the maximum rights of the individual and minimum state interference in the economy and society (*laissez-faire*). They opposed the authoritarian and arbitrary rule of monarchy, and supported the right of individuals to choose their own government, to have freedom of speech and of the press, to own property and acquire wealth. Classic liberalism was in the political centre. Today, liberalism is on the right. It wants to limit the role of the state and promote unregulated competition. It rejects any state responsibility for the provision of welfare or job creation.

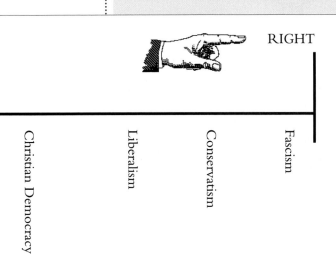

RIGHT

Christian Democracy

Liberalism

Conservatism

Fascism

Conservatism is the belief that society's institutions and traditions should be preserved and respected. It believes that political, economic and social inequality reflects inevitable differences between people's abilities and wealth. It believes in strong, central government but with individuals as independent as possible. Change is justified only where clearly necessary.

Fascism is the belief in a single-party, authoritarian political system where the individual is totally subordinate to the state. It is often combined with extreme nationalism, usually expressed as racism and anti-semitism. Fascism is openly anti-democratic, believing the interests of workers and business are best served by a highly centralised 'corporate' state. Today, neo-fascism has regained popularity across Europe. It claims that immigrants and ethnic minorities are the cause of economic problems and unemployment.

Christian democracy is conservatism but closely identified with the defence of morality and sometimes of the Church, either Protestant or Catholic. It favours an unregulated economy but with a commitment to social justice.

Nationalism can be either on the left or on the right. It is the belief that each nation (people sharing similar ethnic background, language, culture, etc) should have its own political system. On the right, nationalism can be linked to racism, the belief that different races are unequal. People seek to create one nation by excluding or annihilating other national groups. Under Hitler, six million Jews were killed in gas chambers. In Bosnia, thousands of Muslims were killed under a policy that became known as 'ethnic cleansing'. Across Europe today, many people are refused entry into countries because of their national origin. On the left, nationalism is linked to the struggle for independence and self-determination. These national liberation movements are often influenced by communism or socialism because their aim is to eliminate the exploitation of a native population by a large colonial power.

ASSIGNMENTS

1   Write a description of one of the political ideologies shown on pages 132 and 133 in your own words.
    (a) What are the main beliefs and objectives?
    (b) Which group(s) of people do you think would support these ideas and why?
    (c) Which group(s) of people do you think would oppose these ideas and why?
2   What does the term 'political equality' mean?
3   What does the term 'equality of wealth' mean?
4   How would you describe the political ideology of the Greens?
5   Which views are critical of communism but still agree with many of the ideas of Marx?
6   Which political views have been associated with defence of the monarchy?

7   These are terms which you often hear on radio or read in the newspapers.
    How would you explain each of them? Use a dictionary to help you.
    (a) authoritarianism
    (b) racism
    (c) anti-semitism
    (d) defence of customs and tradition
    (e) as little interference as possible by government in people's lives
    (f) moral beliefs
    (g) mass appeal
    (h) consumerism
    (i) egalitarianism
    (j) welfare state
    (k) public ownership
    (l) capitalism.
8   Jean-Marie Le Pen, Hitler, Mussolini and Franco all support which political
    ideology?

ACTIVITIES
1   Collect policy statements from all the Irish political parties. Using the summary of
    political ideologies on pages 132 and 133, identify the Irish parties according to
    their ideology.
2   What were some of the reasons for the failure of communism?
3   Organise a classroom discussion on unemployment. Each student or group of
    students should represent a different political viewpoint.
4   Listen to a political discussion on television or radio. Identify the political point of
    view of each of the speakers.
5   Organise a classroom discussion: Thomas Paine advocated political equality while
    Marechal spoke of equality of wealth. What is the difference?
6   Identify the political views of the following political parties according to the
    left/right spectrum on pages 132 and 133. Look through a recent newspaper to
    find additional political parties.
    (a) Conservatives (UK)
    (b) Democrats (USA)
    (c) National Front (UK)
    (d) African National Congress, ANC (South Africa)
    (e) Christian Democrats (Germany).

FOUNDATIONS OF THE IRISH PARTY SYSTEM

Most of Ireland's political parties stem from the same origin. Over the decades, political parties have split and new ones have been formed because of differences over the commitment to national unity, economic priorities, the needs of small farmers or workers, and disagreement with paramilitary activities.

The split over the signing of the Treaty with Britain in 1921 and the resulting Civil War (1922-23) have been credited as the sole basis of difference between Fianna Fáil and Fine Gael. According to this view, differences on economic or social issues have been less important. Both parties emphasise this factor by using historical imagery in their names: Soldiers of Destiny (Fianna Fáil) and Tribes of Érin (Fine Gael).

Other commentators claim that social and economic differences or social bases have always existed between the political parties. According to this view, each of the parties represent different social groups. Consequently, each offers different solutions. FG was supported in the 1920s by large farmers and businesses who wanted to maintain (trade) relations with Britain. In contrast, FF represented 'the man of small property' who wanted to fight for full independence.

Labour was founded by the trade union movement to push for political and economic change even though Ireland was an agricultural country without a sizeable urban working class. It is the oldest political party in the state but until recently it has played a minor political role. In contrast, three attempts to form a political party for farmers had little electoral success. Farmers have been more influential through their farming organisations such as the IFA and the ICMSA.

In recent decades, distinctions based on ideological views have become more important. Voters are less influenced by 'which side' their fathers or grandfathers fought on during the Civil War. Today, voters are more likely to choose between politicians of different parties, depending upon the policy options offered. The Green Party emerged out of public concern for the environment. Christian Solidarity, Solidarity and Muintir na hÉireann represent people who believe society should promote moral values.

Today, six political parties are represented in the Oireachtas: Fianna Fáil, Fine Gael, the Labour Party, Progressive Democrats, Democratic Left and the Green Party. There are also several politicians who belong to no political party and are known as Independents.

IRISH POLITICAL PARTIES SINCE 1900

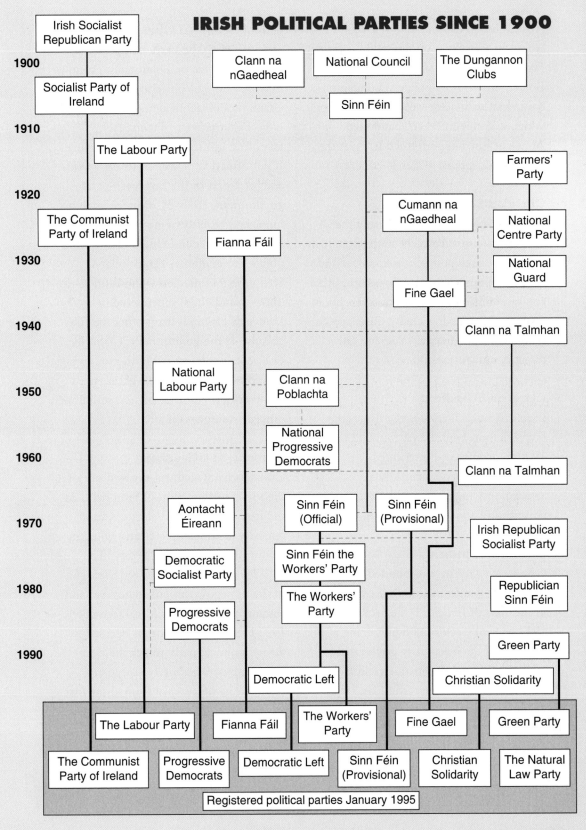

Aontacht Éireann

Aontacht Éireann was founded by a former Fianna Fáil TD and minister, Kevin Boland, in 1971. Its policy was based on traditional nationalist views on unification which it claimed FF had abandoned. Aontacht Éireann performed badly at the polls and disappeared after 1976.

Christian Solidarity Party

Christian Solidarity Party, formerly the Christian Centrist Party, believes strongly in fundamental religious/Catholic values and ethos. It opposes abortion, divorce, artificial contraception and sex education in schools. Its support is growing among those people who feel that traditional values are under threat in modern Ireland.

Clann na nGaedheal

Clann na nGaedheal was the first name given to Sinn Féin. It was founded in 1900 to promote cultural and economic independence. Any association which accepted its constitution and aims could join.

Clann na Talmhan

Clann na Talmhan was founded in 1939. Its support was from among small farmers in the west of Ireland. It did well in the 1943 general election. Despite being a member of the inter-party government, 1948-51, its vote declined. Eventually its members joined other parties. By 1965, Clann na Talmhan had ceased to exist.

Clann na Poblachta

Clann na Poblachta was formed in 1946 and was led by Seán McBride, a former IRA chief of staff. Many of those involved with the party had previously been to the fore of a nationalist group called Coras na Poblachta (1940-45). Clann na Poblachta aimed to be a radical alternative to Fianna Fáil, favouring unification and social policies. It performed very well in its early years, and took part in the first inter-party government, 1948-51. One of its two ministers, Noel Browne, introduced the famous 'mother and child' scheme, and policies to eradicate TB in Ireland. Religious and medical opposition to the 'mother and child' scheme led to Browne's dismissal from office and the collapse of the government. Clann na Poblachta's support fell in the following elections. Although some of its members joined other parties, it did not officially merge with any.

Cumann na nGaedheal

Cumann na nGaedheal evolved out of the pro-Treaty faction of Sinn Féin. At the June 1922 general election, the majority of the people clearly voted in favour of accepting the Treaty. The anti-Treaty group challenged the right of the new government to govern, and abstained from the Dáil. In December 1922 Pro-Treaty supporters decided to form a political party under the leadership of William T. Cosgrave. Cumann na nGaedheal formed the first government of the Irish Free State with Cosgrave as president of the executive council, a post similar to that of the Taoiseach today. It lost power in 1932 to Fianna Fáil.

Democratic Left

The Democratic Left was formed in 1992 when six TDs and one MEP left the Workers' Party due to differences over the party's future direction and continued speculation over links with paramilitary activities in Northern Ireland. Democratic Left is a democratic socialist party with support coming primarily from urban working-class constituencies. It did poorly in the 1992 general election, but gained two seats in by-elections against the odds. In December 1994 it joined a coalition government with Fine Gael and the Labour Party following the sudden collapse of the FF/LP coalition.

Democratic Socialist Party

The Democratic Socialist Party was formed in 1982. It advocated secularism (separation between church and state) and recognised the desire of the majority in Northern Ireland to remain within the United Kingdom. Jim Kemmy was their only TD. In 1990, the party merged with the Labour Party.

Farmers' Party

The Farmers' Party was formed in 1919 as the political voice of large farmers and the Irish Farmers' Union. It successfully contested elections in 1922, 1923 and 1927. In the 1932 election, its leader and two other TDs stood for Cumann na nGaedheal. Others merged with the National Centre Party.

Fianna Fáil

Éamon de Valera founded Fianna Fáil in 1926, having provoked a split in Sinn Féin over its abstentionist policy (it refused to enter the Dáil despite winning seats). Since 1932, Fianna Fáil has been the largest political party in the country and has dominated government. It successfully wins support in both rural and urban areas and from all social classes. It has located itself in the political centre, promoting policies of both right and left, depending upon the political situation. Officially it is known as Fianna Fáil The Republican Party. By the 1980s, economic and social change in Ireland undermined FF's support. Its reluctant formation of a coalition with the Progressive Democrats in 1989 paved the way for a partnership government with Labour in 1993. This was a formal recognition that FF would have difficulty holding power on its own in the future.

Fine Gael

Fine Gael was formed in 1933 with the bulk of its membership drawn from Cumann na nGaedheal. It had strong associations with the fascist Blueshirts in the 1930s. In the 1980s, under Garret FitzGerald, it affiliated to the right-of-centre Christian Democrats in the European Parliament and developed a more liberal image. It is considered the main opposition party to Fianna Fáil, but has only held power in coalition governments. Its support comes primarily from the urban and rural middle class, and from large farmers.

Green Party

The Green Party was born from the ecology movement and the Green Alliance of the 1970s. It was formed in response to growing public concern about the local and global environment. In 1981 it became the Ecology Party of Ireland, and changed its name in 1988 to the Green Party/Comhaontas Glas. It won a single Dáil seat in 1989 and again in 1992, and several urban-based local authority seats in 1991. It performed very well in the 1994 European elections, topping the poll in Dublin. Its support comes mainly from young, middle-class voters.

Irish Republican Socialist Party

The Irish Republican Socialist Party was formed by several people who left Official Sinn Féin over the latter's rejection of paramilitary activity. It established its own military wing known as the Irish National Liberation Army (INLA) in Northern Ireland.

Irish Socialist Republican Party

The ISRP was founded by a small group of socialists in May 1896. It was strongly influenced by James Connolly's view that a social revolution was needed to bring about Irish independence and a society that would benefit small farmers and workers.

National Centre Party

The National Centre Party emerged as a national party from an amalgam of the National Farmers' and Ratepayers' League in 1932. In September 1933 it joined with Cumann na nGaedheal and the National Guard to form the United Ireland Party, which was reconstructed as Fine Gael.

National Council

National Council was the name of Arthur Griffith's organisation. It favoured an Irish independent state linked to Britain by the monarchy, although home rule might be acceptable.

National Guard

In 1932 the Army Comrades Association was formed. It was renamed the National Guard in 1933. It was commonly known as the Blueshirts because of the uniform shirts they wore in the fashion of the fascist Blackshirts in Italy and Brownshirts of the Nazis. General Eoin O'Duffy was the leader of this group.

National Labour Party

In 1944 the National Labour Party (NLP) was formed following a split in the Labour Party. The NLP accused the Labour Party of being infiltrated by communism. Some also opposed 'Big Jim' Larkin who had been expelled and then readmitted to the Labour Party. It supported the inter-party government of 1948. It rejoined the Labour Party in 1950.

National Law Party

Natural Law Party believes that 'transcendental meditation' will bring peace and harmony to society. It contests elections but has negligible support.

National Progressive Democrats

National Progressive Democrats was founded in 1958 by two former Clann na Poblachta TDs, Noel Browne and Jack McQuillan. Early on, there was a split and neither TD tried to build up the party. In 1963 Browne and McQuillan joined the

Labour Party and announced that the NPD had been disbanded.

Progressive Democrats

The Progressive Democrats were formed in 1985 by former FF and FG politicians. The PDs quickly attracted much popular support among the urban middle classes. The party is considered to be on the political right economically. However, it is closer to the left on social issues. Between 1989 and 1992, it was in a coalition government with Fianna Fáil. It is the first Irish political party to have a woman leader.

Republican Sinn Féin

Republican Sinn Féin split from (Provisional) Sinn Féin in 1986 in order to pursue more traditional nationalist goals. There are claims that it has a paramilitary wing.

Sinn Féin

Sinn Féin was founded in 1908 when Clann na nGaedheal, the Dungannon Clubs and the National Council merged. It favoured cultural and economic self-reliance. Its name, given to it by Máire Butler in 1905, described its views: 'ourselves alone'. Although it became the most influential Irish nationalist 'movement', it was not very important until after the 1916 Easter Rising. It was the major force behind the establishment of the Irish Republic and the First Dáil in 1919. After the treaty was signed ending the War of Independence from Britain in 1921, Sinn Féin split into two organisations. Those who favoured the treaty became Cumann na nGaedheal, and those who opposed it retained the name Sinn Féin. In 1926, Éamon de Valera left and formed Fianna Fáil. Sinn Féin continued its military campaign for total Irish independence. In 1970, it split into Provisional Sinn Féin and Official Sinn Féin.

Sinn Féin (Official)

When Sinn Féin split in 1970, Official Sinn Féin became increasingly involved in political rather than paramilitary activities. In recognition of this new focus, it changed its name in 1977 to Sinn Féin the Workers' Party.

Sinn Féin (Provisional)

Sinn Féin (Provisional) is the political arm of the IRA although this distinction is not always clear. As such, it concentrated on forcing the British out of Northern Ireland by military means. It is strongest in Northern Ireland, where its leader Gerry Adams won a seat in the House of Commons in 1983 although refused to take it up. It abandoned **abstentionism** in the Republic in 1986 to capitalise on the 1981 election when two 'H-Block' candidates won Dáil seats in border constituencies. They now hold only local government seats. In Northern Ireland the party represents about 10 per cent of the nationalist community. In 1994 Adams convinced the organisation of the need to abandon violence and support the Joint Declaration for Peace and Reconciliation. An IRA ceasefire was declared on 31 August, 1994.

abstentionism:
the refusal to take up a seat in parliament even though the person has been elected

Sinn Féin the Workers' Party
Sinn Féin the Workers' Party was the name given to Sinn Féin (Official) in 1977 to illustrate its move away from paramilitary and towards political activity. During this period, the party modelled itself on east European communist parties. In 1982 it became The Workers' Party.

Socialist Party of Ireland.
The Socialist Party of Ireland was founded in 1904 but remained a small organisation. It was reorganised in 1909. James Connolly was its most influential member.

The Communist Party of Ireland
The Communist Party of Ireland was a successor to James Connolly's Socialist Party of Ireland. It was most influential during the 1930s when it opposed the Blueshirts as a form of Irish fascism. Some of its members formed the Connolly Brigade, a section of the International Brigade, to fight the rise of Franco during the Spanish Civil War (1936-7). James Larkin, famous for his leadership of the Dublin lock-out in 1913, won a seat for the CPI in 1927. Michael O'Riordan has been its most influential leader.

The Dungannon Clubs
The Dungannon Clubs were founded in the north by Denis McCullough and Bulmer Hobson to promote the formation of an independent Irish republic.

The Labour Party
Founded in 1912, the Irish Labour Party was formed as the political party of the Irish Trades Union Congress to represent the interests of working people. Thomas Johnson was its most influential leader at this time. In 1930 it formed a separate organisation. It supported de Valera in 1932. Between 1948-87, it formed four coalition governments with other parties to keep Fianna Fáil out of government. In 1992 it formed a government with Fianna Fáil against all the odds. That government collapsed suddenly in November 1994. Then it negotiated a left-of-centre government with Fine Gael and Democratic Left.

Recently Labour has won increasing support among the liberal and urban middle class. It is a social democratic party, to the left of centre.

The Workers' Party
The Workers' Party was the only political party to organise on an all-Ireland basis. It aimed to become the left alternative to the Labour Party. Its support came primarily from among the urban working class, with political success confined primarily to the Republic. Its break-through came in the 1985 local and 1989 general elections due in large measure to constituency activity. Continued allegations and media evidence of the existence of the Official IRA and relations with communist governments in eastern Europe and North Korea led to a split in the party. The bulk of the membership in the Republic left to form the Democratic Left in 1992. In the general election of that year, it lost its sole Dáil seat. While the WP retains a presence in Northern Ireland, it has all but disappeared in the south.

ASSIGNMENTS

1   Identify the following Irish political parties:

(a) Which party was a major force behind the establishment of the First Dáil in 1919?

(b) Which party has widespread support from both urban and rural areas and from all social classes?

(c) Which party has been in coalition governments with both Fianna Fáil and Fine Gael?

(d) Which party was the first to elect a woman as its leader?

(e) Which party describes itself as 'democratic socialist' and won two by-elections in 1994?

(f)   Which party is affiliated to the Christian Democrats in the European Parliament?

(g) Which party was formed because of public concern about the environment?

(h) Which party is described as the political wing of the IRA?

2   List the Irish political parties which have been formed to promote each of these objectives:

(a) national unity

(b) economic priorities

(c) the needs of small farmers

(d) the needs of unemployed and workers

(e) disagreement with paramilitary activities.

RESEARCH ACTIVITIES

1   Write an essay on the history of one of Ireland's political parties. Use primary sources, such as newspapers and autobiographies, to give a fuller picture of the events and people involved.

2   Write a profile of one of the following Irish political leaders: W.T. Cosgrave, Michael Collins, Éamon de Valera, Thomas Johnston, Eoin O'Duffy, John A. Costello, Noel Browne, Seán McBride, Seán Lemass, Charles Haughey, Garret FitzGerald, Dick Spring, Albert Reynolds, Proinsias de Rossa, Mary Harney, John Bruton and Bertie Ahern.

ACTIVITIES

1   Collect information from as many of the Irish political parties as possible. Organise a role-play of the Dáil session. Groups of students should represent each of the political parties.

2   Interview a local politician about his or her views on an issue of concern to the class.

3   Organise a Question and Answer forum in your school with local politicians from both local and national government.

IRISH POLITICAL PARTIES IN A EUROPEAN CONTEXT

Compared with political parties elsewhere in Europe, the differences between Irish political parties is not always clear. They are often reluctant to describe themselves as conservative, liberal or socialist. This can make it confusing for the public.

Since Ireland joined the European Community in 1973, we have elected political representatives or **MEP**s to the European Parliament (EP) every five years. MEPs sit and conduct business in the EP according to their membership of a political group. These political groups correspond to the major political ideologies discussed on pages 132 and 133.

While Irish politicians may be reluctant to identify their views at home, they must do so in the European Parliament. The diagram of the Parliament on page 177 shows the distribution of seats according to political grouping as of the 1994 European election. Can you locate the Irish MEPs? What are their political views?

MEP:

Member of the European Parliament

Bertie Ahern, TD.

IRISH POLITICIANS

Politicians are people engaged in politics. In all democratic societies, politicians are elected by the public to act as their representatives and vote on their behalf. They contest elections on the basis of their party affiliation, their activity in the constituency, their personality and/or their family background.

There are 226 politicians in the Oireachtas (166 in the Dáil and 60 in the Seanad), and 1,622 members of all the local authorities (county council, corporation, urban district council, town commissioner). Approximately 80 per cent of TDs, and 60 per cent of Senators are also members of at least one local authority while several have been members of the European Parliament.

There is no constitutional or legal restriction on the number of 'seats' to which a politician may be elected. However, you cannot hold membership of the Dáil and the Seanad at the same time.

There is much controversy about being a member of more than one elected body (**dual mandate**) because it is believed that:

(a) politicians cannot properly represent the public given the work load and number of meetings at local, national and European level

(b) political representation is exclusive to a small number of powerful people

(c) it sends the wrong signals to the public because it is seen as 'double jobbing' and greedy.

Most politicians begin their careers dealing with local problems of housing,

dual mandate:

being elected to more than one elected office at the same time

health, education, amenities, roads and traffic, and planning and development. People like to be able to contact their politicians easily and know that their politicians are active and knowledgeable about community concerns. Membership of local authorities, health boards, vocational education committees, agricultural committees and harbour commissioners is one of the most important ways for politicians to extend their knowledge, influence and popularity.

Even after election to the Oireachtas, politicians need to maintain this contact. Failure to do so would almost certainly result in the loss of the seat. This is not just an Irish phenomenon. The motto of Tip O'Neill, a former Speaker of the US House of Representatives, the most powerful position in the Congress, was: 'All politics is local'.

'Localism' is an important path to election. Although there is no residency requirement for election, most TDs live in or near their constituency. Senators are elected according to different criteria but close contact with a constituency is required if they wish to become TDs.

Politicians come from various backgrounds but all pursue a similar path to election. Most are members of a local authority. Others participate in sports (GAA), farming organisations, trade unions, trade associations, and community and voluntary groups. A few have been members of cultural, religious or social organisations.

The Lemass family is one of the most famous political families. This photo shows two Taoisigh (Seán Lemass and Charles Haughey), Noel Lemass (a junior minister), his wife Eileen (a TD and MEP), and Seán Haughey (a TD).

TDs are relatively young by international standards. Their most common occupations are as teachers, solicitors, business people and farmers. In contrast, politicians from small farming, working-class or unemployed backgrounds are rare. The majority of TDs have a third-level education. Some have fathers or other relatives who were also politicians. Like Irish society, the overwhelming majority are Catholic; politicians from Protestant, Jewish, Muslim or no religious beliefs are in the minority. Women have been seriously under-represented in politics at both national and local level. However, the signs are that this situation is now changing.

The following figures are from the 27th Dáil, elected November 1992.

TDs who are related to former and serving deputies

as sons	20
as daughters	4
as nephews	6
as nieces	2
as grandsons	5
as granddaughters	1
as brothers	4 pairs
as brother and sister	1 pair

Main occupations of TDs

teachers/lecturers	38
farmers	23
company directors/business	23
lawyers	16
clerical and technical	15
science and engineering	9
accountants	8
trade union officials	5

In recent years, voluntary community groups, sporting groups, residents' and tenants' associations, youth groups, etc. have played a more important role in society. Occasionally, candidates supporting a local school, hospital or sports complex, or opposing potholes in roads have won seats in the Dáil.

Membership of sports and social clubs

GAA	43
Soccer	11
Rugby	9
Golf	6

Of those questioned, none of the women TDs said she was a member of the GAA.

Membership of other organisations

Amnesty International or CND	12
Earthwatch or Greenpeace	3
Conradh na Gaeilge	2

RESEARCH ACTIVITY

Who are the following politicians?

(a) I am the longest serving TD.

(b) I had the highest number of first-preference votes in the country at the last election.

(c) I was the first TD to publish a book of poetry.

(d) I was appointed to the cabinet on my first day in the Dáil.

(e) I was a member of the cabinet but not a TD.

(f) I was the first female member of the cabinet.

(g) I was the first Taoiseach to have won a number of All-Ireland medals (GAA).

(h) I was president of the Football Association of Ireland.

(i) We were the first brother and sister to be elected.

(j) I was involved in two historic election counts: the longest in the history of the state, and the first in 50 years where the smallest party won a by-election.

(k) I was elected to the Dáil because of popular anger over poor hospital facilities.

ASSIGNMENTS

1 Why do you think there are so few politicians who are women, shift-workers or unemployed?

2 Why do you think so many TDs are members of sports and social clubs?

3 Write for and against the motion: The 'dual mandate' is beneficial because it helps politicians keep in touch with national and local issues.

4 In the Oireachtas, should politicians represent the interests of their local constituency or consider the interests of the entire country?

POLICY-MAKERS OR SOCIAL WORKERS?

The Irish for Dáil Deputy is 'Teachta Dála' or TD. *Focloir Gaeilge-Béarla* gives two translations for the word 'Teachta'. It may mean messenger, envoy, representative or deputy. These two meanings highlight a controversy over the role and function of Irish politicians.

Should TDs be: (a) policy-makers, proposing and debating legislation or (b) social workers, helping with medical, housing or other problems?

To help TDs keep in touch with constituents, most politicians hold weekly advice centres, commonly known as 'clinics'. Since the level of inequality in Irish society is very great, people in most need often turn to their politician for help with housing, medical cards, hospital treatment, employment or grants. In return, politicians hope that the people they help will vote for them. The practice of encouraging constituents to visit politicians for this purpose is called 'clientelism'.

The political commentator Basil Chubb said that TDs went about 'persecuting public servants on behalf of their constituents'. This view claims that Irish politicians are far too busy trying to sort out people's problems and holding advice clinics and have little time to pay attention to national issues. In other words, politicians tend to be social workers rather than policy-makers.

When you go shopping, you feel that people are looking at you. It makes you a little conscious of yourself ... People feel because you're a TD, they can say what they like to you ... At the beginning I was nice to people, polite all the time; now I talk back to them; if they don't like it, they can lump it ... I'm the only TD who doesn't go to funerals – only of close friends who are important to me. I think going to funerals of people you don't know is cynical and wrong ...

Dr Moosajee Bhamjee, Labour TD for Clare, *Evening Herald*, date 1993

... what business is it of a TD to become involved in minutiae on behalf of constituents?
The Irish Times, Editorial, 10 July 1992

Local and individual problems are very much inter-related with the legislative programme ... Passing legislation is not the end of any story.
Pádraig Flynn, former Minister and now member of the European Commission
The Irish Times, 26 September 1989

Many commentators are critical of clientelism. They claim that this system puts about the view that only politicians can solve people's problems. Others have said that it provides an important link between constituents and elected politicians. After all, politicians are elected to represent the needs of all the people in the constituency. The answer probably lies somewhere in between. Few politicians are willing to risk not holding clinics for fear of electoral defeat.

ASSIGNMENT
Draw up a job specification for a TD.

HOW IRELAND VOTES

THE RIGHT TO VOTE

Ireland is a democracy. This means that its citizens are responsible for making decisions about their society. They must, therefore, be active members of society, not just self-interested individuals. The primary way for people to participate in decision-making is to choose a government. This is done by voting.

In Chapter 2, 'Politics and Government', you were introduced to the four fundamental principles of democracy. Two of these principles concern the task of choosing a government. They are:

- **popular sovereignty/popular representation**: government is regularly elected to represent the people in whom the authority to govern resides

- **free, universal and equal suffrage:** the entire adult population has the right to vote, irrespective of wealth, social status, religion, race, gender or mental and physical capacity, in secret and without intimidation or fear.

The right to vote did not always exist. The struggle for the right to vote – the right of franchise – has taken centuries to achieve. Many countries have excluded or restricted people from voting for reasons of race, religion, gender (being female), mental or physical capacity, property ownership, or literacy. People have died and been imprisoned in pursuit of what is now considered a basic human right. Those who hold power through wealth, inheritance, violence or godliness do not want the political system changed.

Today, fear of intimidation, violence or death prevents many people from voting for whom they wish, or in fact from voting at all. Even people in developed societies like Ireland are often prevented from voting because of ignorance, disability, illness, imprisonment or rural isolation.

Election leaflet (1954).

RIGHTS OF CITIZENS

The right to vote is only a small part of citizenship. People argue that without full participation and equality of opportunity in society, the right to vote is meaningless and irrelevant. The following three examples from the USA, South Africa and Communist states, show how people have exercised their rights as citizens.

USA 1964

Black people were denied the right to vote in some southern states because they could not pass a literacy or civic test. The civil rights campaign began when a black woman, Rosa Parks, refused one day in 1955, to sit at the back of a bus in Montgomery, Alabama. She refused to accept discrimination. Led by Martin Luther King (1929-68), campaigners participated in sit-ins, boycotts and protest marches to pursue their objectives. A voter registration campaign taught people how to vote and made sure they were on the voters' register. Finally, the 1964 Civil Rights Act and the 1965 Voting Act disallowed discrimination in housing, employment and voting because of race, colour or religion.

Sister Rosa
December 1st, 1955
our freedom movement came alive
And because of Sister Rosa you know
we don't ride in the back
of the bus no more.

Now Sister Rosa,
she was tired one day
After a hard day on her job
When all she wanted
was a well deserved rest
Not a scene from an angry mob.

The bus driver said Lady you got to get up
Cause a white person wants your seat
But Miss Rosa said no, not no more
I'm gonna stay right here
and rest my feet.

Chorus:
Yeah, Thank you Miss Rosa,
you were the spark
That started our freedom movement.
Thank you Sister Rosa Parks.

The police came without fail
And took Sister Rosa off to jail
14 dollars was her fine
Brother Martin Luther King
knew it was our time
The people of Montgomery
sat down to talk
it was decided that all God's
children should walk
Until segregation was
brought to its knees
And we obtain freedom and equality.

Thank you Miss Rosa
Chorus

So we dedicate this song to thee
For being a symbol of our dignity.
Chorus

Written by The Neville Brothers and D. Johnson

Nelson Mandela on a visit to Dublin.

SOUTH AFRICA 1994

The white South African government introduced a policy of racial segregation and discrimination called **apartheid** against the majority black Africans in 1948. People opposed this and, led by the African National Congress (ANC), participated in strikes, marches and sabotage.

An international campaign which included the boycott of South African wine, fruit and sports people was organised. In 1990, F. W. de Klerk, the new prime minister, urged reform. He released Nelson Mandela, leader of the ANC from prison after serving 27 years for opposition to apartheid. A new constitution was written, and the first all-race election was held in April 1994. A huge campaign, using videos and television, was conducted to teach people how to vote. It was so successful that people stood in line for days in order to vote. Mandela became the first black president of South Africa.

COMMUNIST STATES

Until the mid-1980s, the communist states of the Soviet Union and eastern Europe were governed in an authoritarian manner. Political dissent was not tolerated and only the communist party could contest elections. In 1985 reforms were introduced by Mikhail Gorbachev, the new premier of the Soviet Union. Open elections were held, the constitution was rewritten, and the communist party forfeited its leading role. Two words were used to explain Gorbachev's reforms: 'perestroika' (reconstruction) and 'glasnost' (greater openness). Ultimately the changes led to the collapse of these societies. From the ruins of the Soviet Union, fifteen states were formed, each holding elections. Elections were also held in Hungary (1990), Poland (1989), Czechoslovakia (1990), Romania (1990), Bulgaria (1990) and Albania (1991).

apartheid:
a system of racial segregation and discrimination introduced in South Africa by the minority white population against the majority black population

ASSIGNMENTS

1 What does the term the 'right of franchise' mean?
2 Who gives an elected government the 'authority to govern'?
3 In a democracy, on what basis can the entire adult population vote?
4 Which group of people do not wish to see the political system changed?
5 On what basis have people been excluded from voting?
6 What tactics did Martin Luther King use to win the right to vote for black people in the USA?
7 By what simple action did Rosa Parks challenge the discrimination laws in the USA?
8 Under the banner of what two words did Mikhail Gorbachev introduce reform into the Soviet Union?

RESEARCH ACTIVITIES

1 Martin Luther King (USA), Mahatma Gandhi (India) and Nelson Mandela (South Africa) were important figures in the twentieth century. Write about one of them. What were their political views?
2 In the 1990s, the Soviet Union split into fifteen independent states. List them.
3 What is the name of the South African government minister who, prior to his appointment in 1994, lived in Ireland and was a leading member of the Irish Anti-Apartheid Movement?

ACTIVITIES

1 Today, fear of intimidation, violence or death prevents many people voting for whom they wish, or in fact from voting at all. Collect material from any of the Irish aid agencies or Amnesty International about this problem.
2 Organise a classroom discussion: In Ireland, the right to vote includes all adult citizens over the age of eighteen years. Citizens of other European Union countries or elsewhere can vote only in local or European elections.
   Do you think the right to vote should be denied by law to any of these people?
3 Look at one of the following films: *Mississippi Burning* (dir. Parker); *Gandhi* (dir. Attenborough); *A World Apart* (dir. Menges), *Cry Freedom* (dir. Attenborough). They tell the story of the struggle for the right to vote and equality in the USA, India and South Africa.

WHO VOTES AND WHY?

While many people around the world are fighting for the right to vote, others refuse or forget to vote. This is because voting is voluntary. In the USA, fewer than half the people entitled to vote actually do so. This means that fewer than 50 per cent of Americans vote for the most powerful politician in the world.

In the 1992 general election in Ireland, only 67 per cent of people eligible to vote did so. This was the lowest turn-out since June 1927. Irish people are even less likely to vote in local government or European Parliament elections.

Some groups of people are more likely to vote than others. People in good jobs or owning property usually vote while those who are unemployed or illiterate may not. In areas of high unemployment and poverty in Ireland, the 'turnout' can be as low as 35 per cent.

People often say: 'If I do not vote, then it won't affect me' or 'The politicians are all the same – nothing ever changes'. However, not to vote creates a vicious circle. If the unemployed or people with alternative views do not vote, then politicians and government are less likely to be interested in their needs and problems.

Elections are often criticised as a waste of money and time. Some people cynically describe it as a 'fashion show'. However, in a democracy there is no alternative to elections. It is the time when politicians must face the public and answer for what they have done or hope to do.

Voting is the most important activity in any democratic society. Everyone, no matter how wealthy or poor, has an equal chance to voice his or her opinion. If you do not vote, then you allow the people in power to always hold power.

Likely to vote	Less likely to vote
• employed men	• unemployed men
• employed women	• women in the home
• middle to high income earners	• low income and people living in poverty
• business and professional people	• unskilled or low skilled workers
• those who work 9am-5pm	• those who work shift, overtime or irregular hours
• well educated people	• early school leavers
• middle-aged (35-55 years)	• young people (under 35 years)
• married people	• single people
• members of organisations	• isolated individuals or loners
• residents in a community	• newcomers to a community
• home owners	• people who rent (either from the local authority or from private landlords)
• people living in private estates	• people living in local authority estates
• members of the majority religion	• members of the minority religion, race or ethnic group
• citizens in crisis situations	• citizens in normal situations

In some countries it is illegal not to vote. Australia and Belgium have compulsory voting; people can be fined for not voting. In other countries, voting takes places on Sundays. This makes it a 'holiday' and allows everyone to get to the polling station. Nevertheless, people who work unsocial hours often find it difficult to vote even though the polling stations are open for twelve hours.

Many countries have a system of postal voting. People who are away, disabled or in hospital may vote by post. In Ireland, postal voting exists only for members of the army and gardaí, and for people registered with a disability or permanently in an institution. Many third-level students are **disenfranchised** because they cannot return home during term. At the moment, Irish emigrants cannot vote in Irish elections although in 1995, the government proposed allowing emigrants to elect three representatives to the Seanad.

disenfranchised:
to deprive a person of their rights of citizenship, e.g. the right to vote

COMPARING ELECTORAL SYSTEMS

There are two main types of electoral systems:

- **Majority systems**: the winner takes all or 'first past the post'. This is the simplest form of counting votes. The person with the most votes or a simple majority wins. There is usually one seat to be filled in each constituency.

- **Proportional representation systems**: seats are distributed according to the proportion or percentage of support won. This system of voting is probably the most 'democratic' because all groups of people in society, even minorities, can win seats. There are usually several seats to be won in each constituency.

MAJORITY VOTING SYSTEMS

- **Simple majority or 'first past the post':** This is the most common. The candidate with the most votes or a simple majority wins. It is used in Britain, Canada and the USA.
- **Absolute majority or the alternative vote (AV):** Voters rank candidates in order of preference. Candidates with the least votes are eliminated and their votes redistributed until one candidate has an absolute majority. This system is used in Australia.
- **Absolute majority with a second ballot:** An absolute majority means that a candidate must receive over half of the votes cast. If this is not reached after the first ballot, a second ballot is held. The candidate with the most votes after the second ballot wins. France uses this system.

PROPORTIONAL REPRESENTATION (PR) SYSTEMS

- **List system:** Each political party draws up a list of candidates. People then vote for their favourite party. If a party receives 40 per cent of the vote, it gets 40 per cent of the seats. Places are filled according to the candidates listed. Sometimes voters can choose their favourite candidate from the list. Most of continental Europe and Scandinavia use this system.
- **Single transferable vote (STV):** Voters rank candidates in their order of preference. Candidates must reach a quota (a set number of votes) in order to be elected. Candidates with the lowest votes are eliminated. Their votes are transferred according to the voters' next preference until all the seats are filled. Often the final seat is filled without anyone reaching the quota. This system is used in Ireland, Malta and Tasmania.

ELECTORAL AND POLITICAL SYSTEMS

The type of voting system a country uses can significantly affect the outcome of elections. The example at the bottom of the page shows how different systems would have altered the general election result of February 1982. That election led to the formation of a minority Fianna Fáil government; Charles Haughey was elected Taoiseach with the support of three independents. This gave Fianna Fáil 84 votes while the combined opposition had 81 votes.

The simple majority system produces clear-cut results: a winner and a loser. Small or local parties are unlikely to do well in this situation. The United States is a good example of this. No other party has successfully competed against the Democrats or the Republicans.

The United Kingdom is an example of how this system can be 'undemocratic'. Look at this example:

- Conservative: 500 votes
- Labour: 499 votes
- Liberal Democrats: 498 votes

The Conservatives have won a simple majority. However, the combined Labour and Liberal vote is greater but their voters are left unrepresented under the simple majority system.

The proportional representation (PR) system elects candidates according to the support they have throughout the constituency. Representation is spread across many political parties and viewpoints. Women and members of ethnic minorities are more likely to be chosen as candidates under this system. In Ireland, a party winning 10 per cent of the vote can often win a seat.

The choice of voting system is often made to favour those in power. PR was introduced in Ireland in 1918 in order to undermine support for Sinn Féin. Since 1973 PR was used in local elections in Northern Ireland to divide unionist support and encourage voting across sectarian lines. In 1959 and 1968, in order to copper-fasten their electoral strength, Fianna Fáil introduced a constitutional amendment proposing to change to the simple majority system. On both occasions people voted against this change.

Today, some Irish politicians prefer the list system. This would benefit parties which have a 'national' profile but would probably adversely affect smaller parties.

Distribution of Seats in the Dáil, February 1982					
	FF	FG	LAB	SFWP	Independents★
Single transferable vote (STV) (actual result)	81	63	15	3	4
If list system were used	84	66	16	0	0
If absolute majority were used	89	57	14	2	4
If simple majority were used	100	53	9	1	3

★Note: includes Ceann Comhairle who is returned automatically
(Notice that neither the Progressive Democrats nor Democratic Left were in existence; Sinn Féin the Workers' Party split into the Workers' Party and Democratic Left in 1992.)

from *Sunday Independent*, February 28, 1982

ASSIGNMENTS

1 What is a constituency?
2 Which group of people often find it difficult to vote? Why do you think this is so?
3 Ireland has a limited system of postal voting. List the types of people you think should be allowed to vote in this way.
4 Who is responsible for the organisation and management of elections?
5 What are the two main types of electoral systems?
6 Which electoral system is used in England and the USA?
7 Which electoral system is used in Italy?
8 Which electoral system is used in Ireland? Why was it introduced here in 1918?
9 Why do you think Fianna Fáil twice favoured changing the voting system?
10 Do you think it would be desirable to change the voting system in Ireland to either the majority system or the list system?

ACTIVITIES

1 Organise a classroom discussion: Look at the list of people who are more likely or less likely to vote. Why do you think these people are listed under these headings? Which other groups of people would you add to each category?
2 Organise a classroom debate: That it should be illegal not to vote.
3 Organise a classroom discussion: Irish emigrants should have the right to vote in Irish local or general elections or both?
4 From your local authority get a copy of the election returns for the most recent election in your city or county. What was the voter turnout for each constituency or ward? Was the voter turnout higher in some areas than in others? Why do you think this is the case?

HOW DOES THE STV SYSTEM WORK?

Bunreacht na hÉireann established the principle of suffrage equality. This means that everyone's vote has the same importance:

> one person = one vote
>
> one vote = one value.

The constitution also outlines guidelines for elections to the Dáil:

- single transferable vote form of proportional representation
- multi-member constituencies with three or more seats
- one TD for every 20,000 to 30,000 people (this ratio to be determined by law)
- constituency boundaries to be re-examined at least every twelve years.

A motion, known as the 'writ', calling a general election, must be introduced in the Dáil between twenty-one and twenty-eight days before polling. The campaign is then seen to formally begin.

Voting usually takes place mid-week. Schools and similar institutions are usually used as polling stations. They normally open from 9am to 9pm. Each voter can only vote in his or her assigned polling station, which must be located in the constituency for which the election is being held.

In Ireland, people can vote in the following elections:

- Local elections to elect representatives to local authorities
- General elections to elect representatives to Dáil Éireann
- By-elections to elect representatives to Dáil Éireann when a seat becomes vacant between general elections
- European elections to elect representatives to the European Parliament.

A **register of electors** is updated every year. It contains the list of all eligible voters. Everyone whose name appears in the register is issued with a polling card when an election is called. It is an offence to 'impersonate' someone by obtaining their polling card.

On the ballot paper, candidates' names appear in alphabetical order, followed by the name of their party affiliation. If a candidate is not a member of a party, then it says Non-Party. No other information is available on the ballot paper.

register of electors:

the official list of all people entitled to vote in a given constituency

159

The STV system is quite complicated. It involves a series of counts, in which voters rank candidates in order of their preference. Candidates who polled the least are eliminated in sequential order. Their votes are then distributed to the remaining candidates according to the second, third, fourth, etc. preference or choice.

Some people feel that their preferences do not really count. However, in a number of recent elections the margin between winning and losing has been very small, with only a handful of votes separating the candidates. The count in the 1992 general election in the Dublin South-Central constituency has become part of political folklore. The counting and recounting of ballot papers went on for ten days. The final outcome of the election was not decided until the 13th count of the third recount when Ben Briscoe (FF) won the last seat by beating Eric Byrne (DL) by five votes. The 12th preference of a few people made a difference in that election.

The ballot paper may not have any mark on it other than the numeric choice of candidate. Some people accidentally spoil their ballot paper by writing an X rather than a number opposite their choice of candidate or by writing the same number twice. There is no provision for writing the name of an alternative candidate. Ballot papers without the official stamp are considered to be invalid. A paper that is considered to be spoiled is also deemed to be invalid, and is withdrawn at the time of counting.

Voting is carried out in a voting booth, in private. After a vote is cast, it is put in a sealed box. Each box holds all the votes for a particular area or number of streets in the constituency. At the close of polling, all the boxes are brought to the count centre by the gardaí. Counting is done manually; there are no plans to introduce electronic voting. Counting may begin after the polls close or on the following day.

Cliffhanger: *Mr Eric Byrne of Democratic Left and Mr Ben Briscoe of Fianna Fáil, whose fate was decided by the recount in the Dublin South Central.*

The election count is organised and managed by either the city sheriff (Dublin and Cork) or the county registrar. It is their job to make sure the election has been carried out in a fair manner and in accordance with the law and the constitution.

Each candidate can bring some people to act as scrutineers or tallymen. Their task is to oversee the entire counting process and make sure it is fair. They also conduct a preliminary count themselves. These figures help give an election prediction. Over the years, such predictions have proven to be extremely accurate. This system is unique and gives Irish elections a great sense of excitement.

Counting is conducted as follows: To be elected, candidates must reach the quota. Any candidate who reaches or exceeds the quota is considered to be elected. The Droop Quota is based on the number of valid votes or votes cast correctly. Spoiled votes are set aside. The quota is calculated as follows:

$$\left. \frac{\text{number of valid votes}}{\text{number of seats} + 1} \right\} + 1$$

For example, if there were four seats to be filled in a constituency, the quota would be calculated like this:

Quota for Cork North-West (1992)
Number of valid votes: 33,337
Number of seats: 3

$$\frac{33,337}{3 + 1} = \frac{33,337}{4} + 1 = 8,335$$

In a by-election, when only one seat is being contested, the quota is calculated in the same way.

The count proceeds by distributing the votes of:

- those who have over the quota or a 'surplus'
- those with the least number.

The distribution is made according to the next preference on the ballot paper. This process continues until all the seats are filled. When only two candidates remain, the one with the highest number of votes wins even if the quota has not been reached.

Seats 3 Quota 8,335	1st Count	2nd Count Transfer of **Hyland's** Votes	3rd Count Transfer of **Fleming's** Votes	4th Count Transfer of **Cashin's** Votes
CASHIN W (Lab)	4,729	+57 4,786	+204 4,786	-4,990
CREED M (FG)	8,034	+27 8,061	+269 8,330	+1,711 10,041
CROWLEY F (FG)	6,642	+13 6,655	+212 6,867	+1,396 8,263
FLEMING D (FF)	3,176	+18 3,194	-3,194	
HYLAND B (Ind)	180	-180		
KELLY L (FF)	4,201	+21 4,222	+912 5,134	+590 5,724
MOYNIHAN, D (FF)	6,375	+15 6,390	+1490 7,880	+545 8,425
NON-TRANSFERABLE		29	107	748

Cork North-West election count, 1992

SEANAD ELECTIONS

Elections to the Seanad are conducted along different lines. This is because the Oireachtas is organised according to the principle of bicameralism. This means that each chamber in parliament must represent different groups in society. In the UK, the House of Commons is directly elected while the House of Lords is composed of members of the nobility and the Church of England. In the US, the House of Representatives is elected according to population while the Senate has two from each state.

In Ireland, the principle of **'vocationalism'** has shaped the way senators are elected. This idea was influenced by Catholic social teaching in the 1930s. It believed in grouping together people who share a common interest or work. Seanad elections are held not later than 90 days after the Dáil is dissolved. The sixty members of the Seanad are elected by STV in the following way:

1. Forty-three represent five major vocational groupings in Irish society.
- education, national language and culture
- agriculture
- industry and commerce
- labour
- public administration and social services.

Candidates are nominated to stand for election in one of the five panels by professional or other organisations, or by members of the Dáil or Seanad. Only local government councillors, out-going senators and in-coming TDs can vote.

2. Six are elected by university graduates.
- three from the National University of Ireland
- three from the University of Dublin.

These were the two third-level institutions in existence at the time of the formation of the constitution. Since then, new institutions have been established. A constitutional amendment was passed in 1979 to include all graduates but no legislation has yet been introduced.

These senators are referred to as independents because they do not belong to a political party.

3. Eleven are appointed directly by the Taoiseach. This provision was introduced by Éamon de Valera to make sure the government always has a majority in the Seanad.

In 1994, unusually a new government was formed without a general election. The government was dependent on the support of the independents to maintain a majority in the Seanad.

These appointments are usually given to politicians who have lost or hope to win Dáil seats. Occasionally they are given to people who have made a contribution to society: the playwright Brian Friel, the environmentalist Éamon de Buitléir and the peace campaigner Gordon Wilson. Such appointments, however, have been made only when the government's majority in the Seanad was secure.

vocationalism:
the belief that society should be organised according to people's occupations rather than by social class

ASSIGNMENTS

1 What is
   (a) a local election?
   (b) a general election?
   (c) a by-election?
   (d) a European election?
2 What happens to your vote if you deface or place an X instead of a number on your ballot paper?
3 What information appears on a ballot paper?
4 Calculate the quota for the following election circumstances:
   (a) a 4-seat constituency where the 35,000 people have voted; of this, 2,500 were declared invalid.
   (b) a by-election where the turn-out in a constituency of 60,000 votes was only 50 per cent; 3,500 votes were invalid.
5 What guidelines does *Bunreacht na hÉireann* lay down for elections?
6 Explain in your own words what the following terms mean:
   (a) writ
   (b) STV
   (c) surplus
   (d) tallymen
   (e) quota
   (f) register of electors
   (g) preference
   (h) transfer
   (i) spoiled vote.
7 Do you think university graduates should be permitted a special vote in Seanad elections?
8 Devise a list of groups which you think should be represented in Seanad Éireann.
9 What is the difference between a valid and an invalid vote?

ACTIVITY

Organise an election count in your classroom.
(a) Count the votes according to each of the electoral systems mentioned on page 156. Compare the different results.
(b) Which system do you think is fairest?
(c) Which one would you prefer?

THE ELECTION CAMPAIGN

he days of mass meetings and outdoor rallies are over. Elections are being won and lost in the media.

Eoghan Harris, *Irish Press*,
26 November 1990

The election campaign occurs three to four weeks prior to voting. During this time, politicians seek to influence the public to vote for them. Using a combination of posters, leaflets, canvassing door-to-door or by telephone, public meetings, coffee mornings, standing outside shopping centres or churches, politicians persuade, flatter and make promises in return for a vote.

Not long ago, a typical Irish campaign involved public meetings outside church gates or in the centre of small towns. Party and family loyalty counted very highly. Great emphasis was placed on personal contact between politicians and voters. The nod, the wink, the handshake said it all.

Today, people get more and more information about what is happening in the world from television. The majority of the population now live in urban areas. Old political loyalties have faded, and commentators talk of the floating or volatile voter. The large political parties hire public relations and advertising agencies to sell politics to voters. Politics is a product to be marketed and sold as butter or cars or clothing. Greater emphasis is now placed on how the candidate looks and performs on television. Politicians have learned to use the media as a means of promoting their image.

Many politicians will seek out a local football club, a school, day centre or factory in order to present the press with a humorous or striking photograph for publication. They may also suggest that some well-known personality supports and endorses their campaign. With this kind of marketing pressure and presentation, individual politicians have little opportunity to discuss issues and policies they would implement in a new government. Election campaigns concentrate less on policies and more on image.

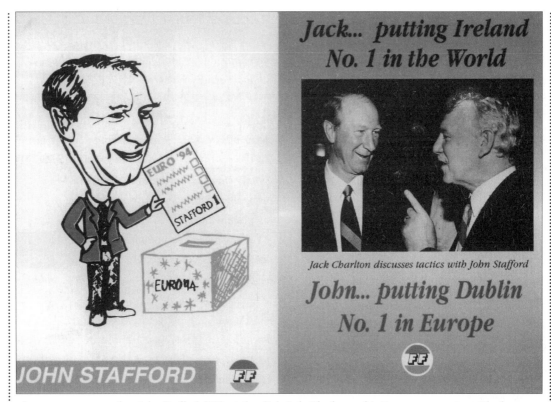

A controversy arose when John Stafford (FF) tried to link Jack Charlton to his European campaign. Charlton denied any endorsement of any candidate.

As a consequence, election campaigns:
- concentrate on personalities
- highlight the party leader
- use family photographs
- create a positive image of the party with soft lenses, music, appeal to emotion
- devise events that will be covered by the news: mass meetings, television debates, press conferences, photo opportunities, and party political broadcasts.

The US presidential election of 1960 is credited as the first television campaign. The debate between John F. Kennedy and Richard M. Nixon demonstrated that a person's appearance on television is more important than what that person says. Kennedy arrived at the television studio well tanned and rested. Nixon, in contrast, was ill and had banged his infected knee getting out of the car. A survey conducted afterwards concluded that those who had seen it on television thought Kennedy had won but those who had only heard it on the radio thought Nixon had won!

In Ireland, the media was exploited for the first time in the 1977 general election. Fianna Fáil hired three advertising companies to present its policies. A song was written, and there were t-shirts, pens and hats. Fine Gael learned the lesson, and in 1981 Garett FitzGerald hired a former marketing director of Yoplait Yogurt to direct the campaign.

Mary Robinson on the day of her presidential nomination.

The Irish presidential election of 1990 shows how an election campaign is shaped. This quotation explains the strategy behind Mary Robinson's campaign.

'Television, as ever, is what counts ... Television can warm up Mary's persona without compromising her three basic strengths: character, calmness and competence ... What Mary needs most of all is for the plain people of Ireland to like her as much as they respect her ... Any classic picture of her in classic clothes conveys this. To this must be added a strong feminine factor. Simply stated her image must be softened – caring and compassion must be added to competence and cool ...

For women Mary should be the kind of woman they want to be; for men the kind of woman they would like to be seen with in public, or to talk to in private ...

Pictures, especially television pictures, determine modern voting. Clothes are critical. You cannot spend too much on good clothes. Classy and classless clothes that speak softly. Ian Galvin at Brown Thomas has a gift for clothes for cameras. Take his advice and don't blink at the bill. It is money well spent.

Eoghan Harris quoted in
Emily O'Reilly, *Candidate*, 1991

President Robinson some months later.

DOES MONEY BUY VOTES?

Election campaigns are about influencing voters. Candidates and political parties publish an election manifesto – a list of what they intend to do if in government. Voters then choose between different policy programmes. The more money spent on glossy leaflets, the more likely they are to attract and win voters.

Candidates and parties are often accused of using large sums of money to buy sporting or other equipment for community associations and youth clubs, or drinks for everyone in the pub. This is called 'vote-buying'. Spending money in this way can also influence voters.

The outgoing government is often at an advantage at election time. During the campaign, it continues to have the authority to make appointments, distribute funds or grants, and approve projects and schemes. Long-awaited school or road improvements will often be announced in a crucial constituency, in what some will see as an attempt to buy votes in order to secure a victory.

How money is raised for campaigns and how it is spent has been controversial for two reasons:

- While lots of money will not guarantee victory, money is an important factor. Smaller parties and independent candidates can be disadvantaged because they usually have less money to spend. Some countries, therefore, limit the amount that can be spent.

- Parties raise campaign funds through contributions from individuals and business. There is, however, a lingering suspicion that donations can influence legislation and policy. The investigation into the Irish beef industry, 1992-94, disclosed that large sums of money had been contributed by various beef companies to Fianna Fáil, Fine Gael and the Progressive Democrats for election expenses. Some countries, therefore, require large contributions to be made public while others countries prefer to fund parties from the national exchequer in order to avoid any doubt.

New legislation in relation to funding of political parties is scheduled to be introduced in Ireland. It will provide that political parties be funded in proportion to the vote achieved at the last election, and will require large contributions to be made public.

... CANDIDATE WHO WILL BE HAPPY TO ANSWER QUESTIONS ON THE AVAILABILITY OF TEE SHIRTS, HAT SIZES, THE STRENGTH OF THE GLUE ON STICKERS AND OTHER ELECTION ISSUES......

ASSIGNMENTS

1   In what way do politicians try to win votes at election time?

2   Why do politicians like to be photographed during a campaign?

3   When was the first 'media election' in Ireland? What effect has it had on subsequent campaigns?

4   Why is campaign funding a controversial issue?

ACTIVITIES

1   Using old newspapers, look at the coverage of the most recent election campaign. Answer these questions:

   (a) How much coverage is given to the election?

   (b) Does the coverage:
       –   highlight the personalities of individual candidates?
       –   explain the issues?

   (c) Which issues are highlighted more than others?

   (d) How much did you learn about the issues from what you read in the newspapers?

   (e) How did the different candidates publicise themselves?

2   Organise a classroom debate: That there should be a limit on how much any political party spends during elections.

3   Organise a classroom discussion: Who manipulates the voter – the media or the political party?

4   Form a political party.

   (a) Outline its political philosophy and policies.

   (b) Design a logo.

   (c) Devise a number of political slogans to be used in a coming general election.

   (d) Write a television or radio script for a party political broadcast.

   (e) Design posters to be used during the election campaign.

   (f) Write a speech to be delivered by the party leader during the campaign.

CHAPTER 9

EUROPE AND INTERNATIONAL AFFAIRS

CHANGING WORLD EVENTS

The twentieth century has been marked by war, revolution and massacres. As a consequence, new political systems have been formed. This century has also been characterised by extraordinarily rapid scientific and technological change, and by improvements in people's quality of life. The following are some major signposts:

- **World War I** was the first global war. It began on 28 June 1914 and eventually involved all the world's major powers. World War II was also a global conflict. Almost all of the world's independent states were involved in some way. The number of people who died or were injured was incalculable. Both wars led to the map of Europe being redrawn and new states being formed.

- The **Russian** or **Bolshevik revolution**, October 1917, produced the first socialist society. It transformed a backward agrarian country and inspired revolutions across Europe and around the world. By 1950, almost one-third of the world's people lived under regimes influenced by Lenin and the events of 1917. The Soviet Union became a super-power. However, by the 1980s, many of the socialist regimes were on the brink of collapse. In 1989, the Berlin Wall dividing socialist East Germany from capitalist West Germany was torn down. Its destruction marked the demise of communism.

- The **rise of fascism**, known as national socialism in Germany and totalitarianism in Italy, was a revolution of the political right. Hitler's triumph was copied by dictators from Latin America to Japan, and by reactionaries in Spain and Portugal. Fascism aimed to overthrow liberal-democratic political institutions. It perpetrated atrocities and the mass murder of millions of Jews, disabled people, homosexuals and trade unionists.

- The **welfare state** was born in the aftermath of the New York stock market crash of 1929. The crash plunged the world into economic chaos known as the Depression. Within months, people lost everything and unemployment sky-rocketed. Wide-ranging social and economic reforms, providing jobs, and unemployment and health benefits were introduced. Between 1947 and 1973, an economic boom transformed the world's economies and people's lifestyles beyond belief. This Golden Age came to an end in the 1970s. Mass unemployment returned, and most of the world's economies have experienced periods of crisis since then.

At the end of the twentieth century, the world is a very different place:

- Europe is no longer the main centre of commercial, intellectual and political power. The USA and the countries of the **Pacific Rim** are as powerful, if not more so.
- The major empires of the nineteenth century no longer exist. Throughout the twentieth century, colonised nations in Africa, Asia, the West Indies and Oceania have won their independence.
- Many people live longer and more comfortably than their parents could have dreamed possible, but many more live in poverty or die from famine and disease.
- The gap between the rich and the poor has widened. The 'third world' lags further behind the 'developed world'.
- The world has become a 'global village'. We can now communicate instantly with any part of the world by telephone, fax or computer.
- Technology has changed the world of work. For example, work which

Pacific Rim:
refers to the economically strong countries of Asia, e.g. Japan, South Korea, China, Malaysia, etc.

traditionally would have been done in Ireland can now be done more cheaply in the Far East, eastern Europe or Latin America. Goods manufactured in one part of the world are sold the next day thousands of miles away.

- Since the collapse of communism in 1989, the world political system has been in a state of uncertainty and change. Across Europe, regional and ethnic conflicts have erupted which threaten the security of the entire continent.

IRELAND AND WORLD EVENTS

Irish people have played a significant part in many of the events and advances of the twentieth century. We have also been strongly influenced by:

- our relations with Britain and the aspiration for 'national unity'
- our membership of European and international political alliances and organisations
- the involvement of Irish missionary and relief work throughout the third world.

Since the foundation of the state, Anglo-Irish affairs have dominated Irish political attention. For many people, reunification of the national territory has been the major issue.

Irish governments have also actively pursued policies that have advanced Ireland's status as an independent country, and brought Ireland into the mainstream of the international community.

During the 1930s, Ireland looked inward,

171

anxious to keep out foreign influences and maintain her independence from the developing European conflict. This reflected Éamon de Valera's belief that 'small states must not become the tools of any great powers'. When Germany invaded Poland in 1939 at the outset of World War II, the Dáil enacted legislation affirming Irish neutrality. The government was given wide-ranging powers to control prices and wages, regulate supplies, and censorship. This period was known as 'The Emergency'.

In the 1950s, Ireland began to turn its attention outwards, joining the United Nations in 1955 and the European Community (now European Union) in 1973. Membership of the European Union plays the most significant role in the daily life of the country. Its institutions may seem distant and remote but it has helped transform Ireland into a modern European state.

Soldiers during Emergency.

ASSIGNMENTS

1   What were the main political and social events that changed the course of twentieth-century history?

2   Write about four ways the world has changed since the beginning of this century.

3   What are the influences that have shaped Ireland's attitudes to world events?

4   The Jewish people were the main victims of Nazi atrocities. Which other groups were also victims? Why do you think these people were selected?

5   What was the Irish government's reaction to the invasion of Poland by Hitler in 1939?

6   What does the term 'global village' mean?

RESEARCH ACTIVITIES

1 List the regional and ethnic conflicts that have erupted in Europe since the collapse of communism.

2 Write an essay about the way one of the events of the twentieth century has affected Ireland.

3 Many Irishmen fought in the Spanish Civil War, 1936-39. Some formed the Connolly Column, part of the International Brigade, to help preserve the Spanish Republic. Others fought on the side of Franco. Write an essay about this.

4 By 1947 Europe was divided by what Winston Churchill called the 'Iron Curtain'. What does this term mean?

5 Read some of the poems of soldiers who fought in World War I: Englishmen Siegfried Sassoon and Wilfred Owens, or Francis Ledwidge who was born in Slane, Co. Meath. Write a paragraph about a poem of your choice.

6 Watch the film *Reds* (dir. Beatty) based on the book *Ten days that shook the world* by John Reed (1919). This book deals with the Russian revolution. Write an essay explaining the reasons for the revolution.

7 Read or watch the film *The Diary of Anne Frank* (dir. Stevens) which tells of the experiences of Anne, her family and friends during the Nazi occupation of Amsterdam. Write an essay on life in Holland at that time.

8 Imagine you were a German boy or girl living in Dresden during the 1930s. Write an essay about the rise of Hitler, from your point of view. Explain your feelings about Nazism.

9 Imagine you were a boy or girl living in Ireland during the 1930s. Write an essay about the rise of Hitler, from your point of view. Remember Ireland was neutral during the war.

10 Draw a map of Europe. Shade in and identify all the states that have been formed from the territory of the former Soviet Union since 1989.

11 Choose one of the nations in Africa, Asia, the West Indies or **Oceania** that won their independence during the twentieth century.
Write an essay explaining what happened.

Oceania:
refers to small countries mainly in the south Pacific

ACTIVITY

Organise a classroom discussion. What are the major world conflicts happening today?
Do any of them present a risk to the rest of Europe? to the rest of the world?
Does Ireland have a role to play in resolving these conflicts?
What can we do?

THE EUROPEAN UNION

At the end of World War II, the world was torn between the ambitions of two superpowers: the Soviet Union (USSR) and the USA. US President Truman called it the 'Cold War'. Europeans turned their attention to establishing a strong European political organisation that would build an economically powerful and united Europe and create a permanent peace.

Over the years, a single integrated political, economic and legal association has developed. Its name has changed to reflect its increased membership and powers. The following treaties trace its development:

- **Paris Treaty**, establishing the European Coal and Steel Community, 1950

- **Rome Treaties**, establishing the European Economic Community (EEC or Common Market) and Euratom (European Atomic Energy Authority), 1957
- **Single European Act**, establishing the European Community, 1987
- **Maastricht Treaty**, establishing the European Union, 1992.

Community law is based primarily on these treaties. They are equivalent to the European Union's constitution.

The European Union is a unique organisation. Unlike other international organisations, European Union decisions take precedence over domestic law. This means that the EU has authority over the internal affairs of its individual member states.

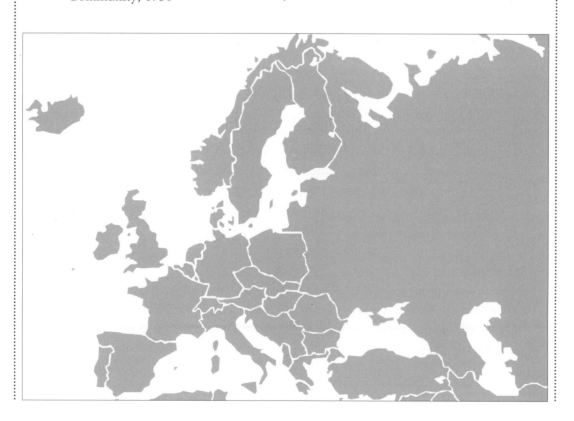

The EU should not be confused with other European organisations. Membership of the following organisations often overlaps with membership of the EU.

- **Benelux** refers to the economic association formed by Belgium, Luxembourg and the Netherlands in 1947. This idea inspired the formation of the EEC.

- The **European Free Trade Association (EFTA)** was formed in 1959 to promote free trade among its members. It was formed by Austria, Denmark, Norway, Portugal, Sweden, Switzerland and Britain. It gained Iceland and Finland but has been considerably weakened by others leaving to join the EU.

- The **Council of Europe** was formed in 1949 to encourage greater unity among member states. Its most important achievement was the establishment in 1950 of the European Convention for the Protection of Human Rights. Decisions of the European Court of Human Rights, which sits in Strasbourg, are binding on signatories to the Convention. Ireland has signed this document. Membership of the Council of Europe includes many non-EU countries.

- The **Organisation of Economic Co-operation and Development (OECD)** began as the Organisation for European Economic Co-operation (OEEC) in 1948. Sixteen European states joined together to rebuild Europe after World War II, using money supplied from the US Marshall Aid Plan. It was renamed the OECD in 1961 when Canada and the USA became full members. Since then, other western countries have joined.

- The **North Atlantic Treaty Organisation (NATO)** was formed in 1948 as the military alliance of the major west European states, Canada and the USA. Its aim is to defend members against attack.

- The **Warsaw Pact** was formed in 1955 by the communist states of eastern Europe to counter the military threat of NATO.

- The **Organisation for Security and Co-operation in Europe (OSCE)** was formed in 1975 as the Conference on Security and Co-operation in Europe. It is concerned with security rather than defence. It was ignored during the Cold War because people were involved with military concerns. Since 1989 there has been renewed interest in the OSCE.

- The **Western European Union (WEU)** was formed in 1954 as a military alliance. It has been called the 'fifth pillar of NATO'. Ireland is not a member but has observer status. Within the WEU, **Eurocorps** was set up as a Franco-German 'battalion'. Some people think the WEU should become a prototype or model for a European army in the future.

HOW THE EU FUNCTIONS

Membership of the EU requires each government to do the following:
- implement directives
- apply regulations
- amend national legislation when necessary.

Failure to comply, particularly with directives or decisions of the European Court, can be hugely embarrassing to the government and ultimately lead to sanctions. Decisions taken 'in Europe' now form the third tier of decision-making in Ireland, after the national government and local authorities.

It was necessary to pass three amendments to the Irish constitution (1973, 1986, 1992) in order to permit decisions of the Commission, the Parliament, the Council and the Court to take precedence over Irish law. In 1973, the Dáil established a committee to keep in touch with European affairs particularly as they affect Ireland. All decisions and documents must be translated and printed in all the official languages of the EU. Irish is not an official EU language.

The European Union functions through a number of institutions, principally through the European Parliament, the European Commission and the European Council.

THE EUROPEAN PARLIAMENT

The European Parliament (EP) is directly elected by each country's electorate (citizens over eighteen years and registered to vote). In January 1995, there were 626 members; fifteen were Irish. The Parliament's term of office is five years. It meets in full or plenary session in Strasbourg once a month.

The main work of the Parliament is done in committees which meet throughout the month. They submit draft resolutions and reports. There are nineteen committees.

The Parliament has power to:
- question the Council, the Commission and the foreign ministers about their activities
- give its opinion on proposed EU legislation
- help draw up the budget, and eventually adopt or reject it
- approve the admission of any new member
- dismiss the Commission.

Members of the European Parliament (MEPs) sit according to their own political party's ideological alignment and not according to their country of origin. The Parliament recognises nine political groups.

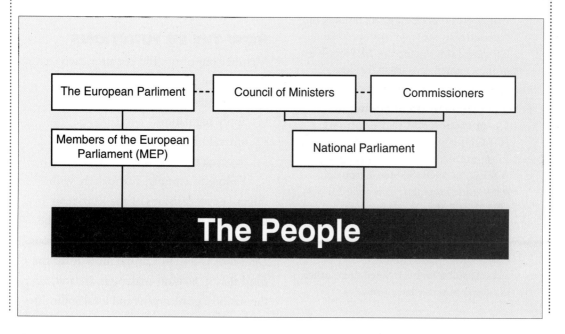

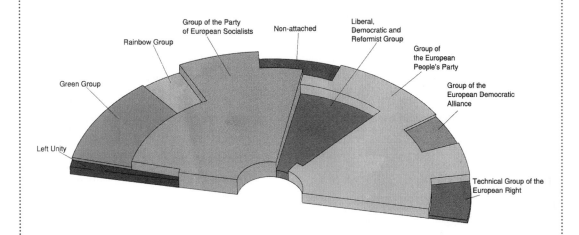

They are listed here according to size:

- Socialist Group
- European People's Party (Christian Democratic Group)
- Liberal Democratic and Reformist Group
- Green Group
- European Democratic Alliance
- Rainbow Group
- European Right
- Left Unity
- non-attached.

THE EUROPEAN COMMISSION

The European Commission is led by twenty commissioners, appointed by their national governments for a five-year term.

Commissioners act on behalf of the European Union not in their own national interest. The Commission is answerable only to the European Parliament.

The Commission has the power to initiate (draft) and execute (implement) laws and budgets. It also has the authority to enforce these decisions. In this way, it acts as the civil service for the EU.

The president of the Commission is formally elected by the European Parliament, although his or her appointment is really the result of political negotiations between the leaders of the member states. It is a very powerful position.

Ireland's EU Commissioners

Patrick Hillery (FF)	1973–1976	Social Policy.
Richard Burke (FG)	1977–1980	Transport, Taxation, Consumer, EP.
Michael O'Kennedy (FF)	1981–1982	President's delegate, Administration.
Richard Burke (FG)	1982–1984	Greek renegotiation.
Peter Sutherland (FG)	1985–1988	Competition.
Ray McSharry (FF)	1989–1992	Agriculture and the CAP.
Pádraig Flynn (FF)	1992–	Social Affairs.

THE EUROPEAN COUNCIL

The European Council comprises the heads of state or government (or other appropriate minister) from all the member states. It became an official body after the **ratification** of the Single European Act in 1986. The Council meets at least twice a year. It lays down the main lines of EU policy.

Depending upon the subject under discussion, the precise composition of the Council may change. For example, when the ministers for foreign affairs from each country meet, they form the Council of Foreign Ministers.

The Council is the ultimate decision-making authority in the EU. It is supposed to reach a unanimous decision. Commission submissions are discussed by the Parliament, reconsidered by the Commission and decided upon by the Council.

The presidency of the Council rotates between the member states in alphabetical order. Each country holds the presidency for six months.

OTHER EU INSTITUTIONS

- **The European Court of Justice** is the highest or supreme court of the European Union. It is composed of thirteen judges and six advocates-general. The court is based in Luxembourg. Its decisions are binding and penalties may be imposed. It interprets EU law and the treaties. It may be called upon to settle disputes between member states or between a member state and the European Commission.

- **The Court of Auditors** monitors how community finances are managed and if they are spent correctly. It audits or inspects the accounts of the EU's institutions and publishes reports on its findings. Large-scale fraud in several member states was discovered by the Court in 1989. The twelve members of the Court of Auditors are appointed by the Council. They, in turn, nominate the president of the Court of Auditors.

- **The Economic and Social Committee** is made up of employers, workers and various interest-group representatives. It has **consultative** status. There are 189 members, each of whom is nominated by his/her own government for a renewable 4-year term. It is organised into sections dealing with particular subjects, e.g. agriculture. Some treaty articles make it necessary for the Council to consult the Economic and Social Committee but its opinions are not binding.

- **The Committee of the Regions** was established in 1993 to involve regional and local authorities directly in decision-making in the EU. There are 189 members, each with an alternate.

- **The European Investment Bank (EIB)** provides finance for projects in all economic sectors of the EU. It also provides loans to third-world countries that have agreements with the EU.

ratification:
the act of agreeing or approving something being done

consultative:
having an advisory role

IMPACT OF EU MEMBERSHIP ON IRELAND

People in Ireland tend to think of the European Union as a dispenser of money. Ireland is a net-beneficiary of EU money. This means it receives more money than it contributes.

Between 1994 and 1999, Ireland will receive approximately £6b for economic development, job training, environmental and structural projects, and Irish agriculture. The money is granted to Ireland because it is one of the poorest or **peripheral** regions of the European Union. It is intended to help Ireland develop to a level broadly in line with the wealthier countries of France and Germany.

Funding from the EU has helped transform our cities and towns, develop our road network, build schools, colleges and ports, dredge waterways, and improve theatres and museums. The government has stated how it intends to spend the money in the *National Development Plan, 1994-99*.

Funding from the EU is channelled primarily through the following programmes:

- **Structural Funds** are aimed at providing financial assistance for major developments – roads, harbours, education and training, industry, etc

- **Common Agricultural Policy (CAP)** is designed to guarantee agreed prices on specified agricultural products, and to provide financial assistance to improve agriculture particularly in the poorer regions of the EU

- **Cohesion Funds** are aimed at providing financial assistance for environmental protection projects and major transportation links in the least prosperous member states.

The impact of European membership on Ireland is, however, much greater than the transfer of funds. It has influenced change in many areas of Irish life: equality in hiring and at work, equal pay, paid maternity leave, social and labour legislation, legalisation of homosexuality, environmental protection, and government spending.

These changes might not have occurred as quickly if left to an Irish government. For example, Irish women had earned less money than men doing the same job and often in the same location. Attempts to remove this inequality had failed until the Commission directed the government to introduce equality legislation. The Anti-Discrimination Pay Act, 1974 and the Employment Equality Act, 1977 require employers to treat all employees equally when hiring, in work and in pay. These laws have gone a long way to establishing equality at work.

peripheral:

those countries which are geographically and economically distant from the major economic and financial centres, which are designated the 'core'

Women outside the Four Courts having won their equality case in 1994.

Social Charter

In 1989, the EU *Social Charter* was adopted. Only the UK refused to sign this document. These twelve principles aim to protect the fundamental rights of citizens, workers, the unemployed, the disabled and the elderly.

1. the right to work in the EU country of one's choice
2. the freedom to choose an occupation and the right to a fair wage
3. the right to improved living and working conditions
4. the right to social protection under prevailing national systems
5. the right to freedom of association and collective bargaining
6. the right to vocational training
7. the right of men and women to equal treatment at work
8. the right of workers to information, consultation and participation
9. the right to health protection and safety at work
10. the protection of children and adolescents
11. a decent standard of living for older people
12. improved social and professional integration for disabled people.

IS EU INFLUENCE FOR THE GOOD?

Obviously people's views of what is good will differ. When the government changed the law to permit homosexual relations between consenting adults in line with a European Court decision, some people argued that 'Brussels' had interfered in Irish affairs. Others saw it as safeguarding human rights.

In Ireland and across Europe, people are debating the pros and cons of a single European currency, the creation of a European army, and the formulation of a common security policy. The UK, for example, opposes any move towards 'federalism' which would make national governments subservient to decisions of the EU. Those who are most vocal in their opposition are called 'Euro-sceptics'.

Irish people have generally been very favourable towards EU membership. The benefits to Ireland were highlighted by the government in 1992 at the time of the referendum on the Maastricht Treaty:

By ratifying Maastricht we will make it possible for Ireland to go on enjoying the very considerable economic benefits of EU membership ... It also offers Ireland very substantial extra benefits ... One of the most important aspects ... is that it lays the basis for economic and monetary union in Europe before the end of the century ... The Maastricht Treaty extends the ability of EU countries to work together on international issues, on matters of common interest to all.

Short Guide to the Maastricht Treaty,
Government Publications, 1992

Others feel that a common approach on international issues poses a threat to Irish neutrality. Ireland has never joined any military alliance, such as NATO or the WEU. Nor has it joined the Non-Aligned Movement, a loose organisation of former colonial or third-world countries formed in 1961 and affiliated neither to the capitalist 'west' nor the communist 'east'.

Whether Ireland should remain neutral is quite a controversial subject. Many people have argued that we can no longer remain neutral in the face of conflicts erupting around the world and especially in Europe. They want to see the development of a common EU security policy, Irish membership of the WEU, and the eventual formation of an EU army. Others do not want Ireland to join any military alliance. They argue that Irish neutrality can make a positive contribution to world peace.

ASSIGNMENTS

1   Why did the leaders of post-war Europe want to build an organisation for 'an economically powerful and united Europe'?
2   Over which law does European Union law takes precedence?
3   Identify the following organisations:
    (a) a military alliance of western European states with America and Canada
    (b) an organisation concerned with security matters within Europe
    (c) an association of non-EU European countries which have signed a 'free trade' agreement
    (d) an institution which established the European Convention for the Protection of Human Rights
    (e) a defence association of communist states.
4   What does EU membership require each government to do?
5   The EU is described as the third tier of decision-making in Ireland. What are the first and second tiers?
6   Which EU institution is answerable only to the European Parliament?
7   Which EU institution meets at least twice a year and outlines policy?
8   Read again the EU *Social Charter*.
    (a) Which rights do you think are the **most** important? the **least** important?
    (b) How do you think the Irish government can ensure that these rights are protected?

RESEARCH ACTIVITIES

1   Look at the map of the Europe on page 174. Identify each member state of the EU and complete the following information for each one:
    (a) name of country
    (b) population (millions)
    (c) currency
    (d) language(s)
    (e) date of joining EU
    (f) head of government
    (g) capital city.

2   Who is/are:
    (a) the EU commissioner from Ireland and his or her area of responsibility?
    (b) the Irish members of the European Parliament, their political party, and the
        political group affiliation of each?
    (c) the president of the European Commission?
3   Why do you think atomic energy was a matter of such concern to Europeans that
    they formed Euratom?
4   Collect information from the European Union office about which Irish laws have
    been influenced by European directives or decisions.
5   Write a paragraph about either Jean Monnet (1888-1979) or Robert Schuman
    (1886-1963), two Frenchmen who drew up plans for a more united Europe.
6   The CAP guarantees prices to farmers for their agricultural produce. Why do you
    think many consumer organisations oppose this policy?

ACTIVITIES

1   Invite one of the Irish MEPs to your class to discuss the workings of the European
    Parliament, and his or her job as an MEP.
2   Organise a classroom discussion: Would a common European army be a good thing?
3   Organise a classroom debate: That Ireland should remain neutral.
4   Each major development project is required to have an environmental impact
    study conducted to assess its effect on the environment. Find out what this
    involves. Have any developments in your area had such a study done? What was
    the result?
5   Invite a representative from the IFA or ICMSA to your class to discuss the farming
    view of the EU.

THE UNITED NATIONS

After World War I, many people believed that war should be outlawed. The League of Nations was formed to establish an international rule of law so that disputes between countries could be resolved before war or armed conflict arose. Ireland joined in 1923 and Éamon de Valera became president of the League Council in 1932.

Unfortunately, the US never became a member. This weakened the organisation from the beginning. The League of Nations was too powerless to prevent invasions by Germany, Italy or Japan of their neighbouring countries during the 1930s. Germany left the League in 1935 and Italy left in 1936.

Towards the end of World War II, the

allies agreed to create a new international organisation to replace the League of Nations. The United Nations Organisation (UNO) was formed in October 1945. The purpose of the United Nations or UN was:

- to maintain international peace and security
- to develop friendly relations between nations based on 'respect for the principle of equal rights and self-determination of peoples'
- to promote international co-operation for solving economic, social, cultural and humanitarian problems.

Today, there are 185 members of the United Nations. Switzerland and the Holy See have observer status. Ireland joined the UN in 1955.

The UN acts as a world government. Its main headquarters is in New York; a second office is in Geneva. It has five main institutions:

- **General Assembly.** It has representatives from all member states. It is the main decision-making body of the UN.
- **Security Council.** It is the main body for keeping international peace and security. There are five permanent members (China, France, the UK, the USA, and the USSR which has been replaced by Russia) plus ten other members. Decisions are generally taken by vote although the permanent members have the right of veto. This system makes sure that the power of the five permanent countries, who were the major victors of World War II, is maintained.
- **Economic and Social Council.** It co-ordinates the activities of the special

agencies of the UN which are involved in economic and social development and co-operation.

- **International Court of Justice.** It is the UN's main judicial body. It gives legal opinion on any case brought before it.
- **Secretariat.** It is the UN's civil service. It is headed by the secretary general who acts both as head of the UN and mediator in international conflicts.

The following men have been secretary general:

- Trygve Lie (Norway) 1946–53
- Dag Hammarskjold (Sweden) 1953–61
- U Thant (Burma) 1961–71
- Kurt Waldheim (Austria) 1971–81
- Javier Peres de Cuellar (Peru) 1981–91
- Boutros Boutros-Ghali (Egypt) 1992–

The UN also sponsors many agencies that work in particular areas. Some of the most well-known are:

- International Labour Organisation (ILO)
- United Nations Educational, Scientific and Cultural Organisation (UNESCO)
- World Health Organisation (WHO)
- International Monetary Fund (IMF)
- International Atomic Energy Agency (IAEA)
- General Agreement on Tariffs and Trade (GATT)
- United Nations High Commissioner for Refugees (UNHCR)
- United Nations International Children's Fund (UNICEF)
- United Nations Relief and Works Agency (UNRWA).

UN PEACE-KEEPING

Irish membership of the United Nations has been an important focal point of our international relations. Ireland has been a long-serving participant of the UN's peace-keeping efforts around the world. We have been involved in more than twenty UN peace-keeping missions to date. The first large-scale mission was with the UN operation in the Congo (now Zaire) in 1960-1964. Most recently, Irish soldiers have served in Bosnia and Somalia. In 1988, UN peace-keepers were awarded the Nobel Peace Prize.

Ireland's contribution to UN missions has included officers, troops and gardaí. The Irish commitment to UN peace-keeping is recognised internationally. Ireland is especially well thought of because of its colonial history and its neutrality. Several force commanders and chief military observers on UN missions have been Irish. Irish volunteers have also acted as UN observers in the first elections in Cambodia and in South Africa. Recently a UN school was established in the Military College of the Curragh Camp, Co. Kildare.

Peace-keeping has proven to be dangerous. A number of Irish soldiers have been killed, most notably in the Congo and in the Lebanon.

The funeral of one of the sixteen soldiers killed in action in the Congo.

RESEARCH ACTIVITIES

1   Find out why Ireland's entry into the UN was blocked by the USSR.
2   The UN is involved in many activities in addition to peace-keeping. List them.
3   Find out more information about any of the UN-sponsored agencies listed above.
4   How do you think Ireland can help promote the aims of the United Nations?
5   List the peace-keeping missions to which Ireland has made a contribution.

ACTIVITY

Organise a classroom discussion: What is the difference between 'peace-keeping' and 'peace-enforcement'? Which do you think the UN should be involved with?

IRELAND AND THE 'THIRD WORLD'

Over the past fifty years, different words and phrases have been used to describe the inequalities between the economic and living standards of countries around the world. The richest countries of western Europe and the USA are said to belong to the 'first world' and the poorest countries to the 'third world'. Others words used are: developing, backward, under–developed, less advanced or primitive.

These words imply that there is a 'pecking order' of superiority among countries in the world. The first-world countries dominate the global economy and exercise real political power. In sharp contrast, many people in the third world are struggling to survive against chronic poverty, famine, disease, poor housing, low income and premature mortality.

In recent decades many people in Ireland have realised that we must involve ourselves in international co-operation; that it is no longer appropriate to isolate ourselves from world events. They believe that our colonial experience, missionary involvement, our own economic problems and our neutrality gives us a unique understanding of third-world concerns. They think Ireland should speak out strongly for justice and equality, and challenge the self-interest of the major world powers when it damages the rights of the world's poor and powerless.

Others disagree. They believe Ireland has its own problems of poverty, unemployment and inequality. Some think Ireland should forge greater links with the powerful countries of the EU instead.

Irish aid agencies, non-governmental agencies (NGOs) and solidarity groups have made a significant contribution to our growing awareness of the third world. The churches have been to the forefront in promoting emergency and development aid programmes and co-operation. Trócaire, Concern, Goal, Gorta and the Church of Ireland Bishop's Appeal send aid workers,

supplies and money. Groups such as Amnesty International, Greenpeace, the Campaign for Nuclear Disarmament and the Irish Congress of Trade Unions are also involved in specific campaigns. Many Irish people volunteer in emergency situations or go abroad as development workers.

In the 1970s, the Anti-Apartheid Movement campaigned against the system of racial segregation in South Africa known as apartheid. As part of the international boycott against South African products, workers in Dunnes Stores went on strike when they refused to handle South African fruit.

Many people are unhappy with the Irish government's response to third-world appeals. For years, Ireland's aid contribution has been one of the lowest in Europe and way below the United Nations' target of 0.7% of **GNP** (Gross National Product). However, in 1995, funding for overseas aid jumped to a record level of £89m.

What can you do? Congood, the Confederation of Non-Governmental Organisations for Overseas Development, lists the following things you can do:
* inform yourself of what the issues are
* write to newspapers or magazines
* join a group or form one in your school
* lobby your local politicians
* fund-raise for projects and programmes
* become involved in issues of justice and development at home
* organise a World Development Week or Day in your school
* invite a speaker to your classroom.

GNP:

the total monetary value of all goods and services produced in a country during a year

THE UNIVERSAL DECLARATION OF HUMAN RIGHTS

Article	Concerns the right to:	It says:
1.	Equality for all	All people have the same dignity and rights.
2.	No discrimination because of: Race Sex Language Religion Political Opinion Property National Origin Social Origin Birth	You should have all the rights and freedom listed in this declaration no matter where you are from, what colour you are, what sex you are, what language you speak, what religion you practice, what views you hold or how rich or poor you are.
9.	Freedom from arrest, detention or exile without reason	No one has the right to put you in prison, or to send you away from your country unjustly.
11.	Be presumed innocent until proven guilty	You are innocent until proven guilty. You have the right to a public trial.
13.	Freedom of Movement	You have the right to travel in your country, to leave it and to return to it.
15.	To a Nationality	You have the right to belong to a country.
17.	Own property	You have the right to own something yourself or share it with other people.
19.	Freedom of opinion Right to seek information and ideas	You have the right to express your thoughts and views freely. No one should stop you from getting information and ideas from other people.
23.	Work Fair Wages Equal pay for equal work Unemployment benefit Join a trade union	You have the right to work and to receive a fair wage. Men and women should receive the same pay for the same work. You have the right to unemployment benefit or social security and to join a trade union.
26.	Education	You have the right to learn. Primary education should be compulsory and free.
29.	Respect of others' rights.	You have duties towards the people you live amongst. In a democratic society, your rights and freedoms shall be limited only as far as necessary to protect the rights and freedoms of others.

From **The Real Guide to Latin America**, *Trócaire*.

ASSIGNMENTS

1 Which countries exercise 'real' political power in the world today?
   Which countries have the least power?
2 Why have Irish people developed an active interest in third-world issues?
3 What is the difference between 'charity' and 'justice' for people living in the third
   world?

RESEARCH ACTIVITIES

1 Denis Goulet, a writer on development issues, lists the following ten points as a
   checklist of development. Choose a country, and investigate how well it meets
   these criteria.
   (a) a healthy, balanced diet
   (b) reasonable medical care for all age-groups
   (c) environmental health and the control of disease
   (d) employment opportunities which ensure the development of talents and skills,
       and guarantee income sufficient for needs
   (e) an educational system which allows for human development, both physical and
       intellectual
   (f) security, freedom of choice and safety
   (g) adequate shelter
   (h) an economic system which values people above profits and efficiency
   (i) a social and political system which actively seeks to end discrimination by class,
       colour, belief or sex
   (j) equality in the degree to which people can exercise control over their lives.
2 If the USA belongs to the 'first world' and Somalia to the 'third world', what is the
   'second world'?
3 Why have the terms 'North' and 'South' been used to indicate the gap between
   the richest and the poorest countries in the world?
4 What do you think are the causes of poverty and under-development in the third
   world?

ACTIVITIES

1 Invite a representative from one of the Irish aid agencies to your classroom to
   discuss the problems of the third world and what Ireland can do to help.
2 Organise a classroom debate: That Ireland cannot afford international aid until our
   own problems are solved.
3 Organise a classroom discussion: Given the level of poverty and inequality in
   Ireland, is Ireland a third-world country?

WOMEN IN
POLITICS

FEMINISM

Throughout history, many people have believed that women are not equal to men. They have claimed that women are not as intelligent as men, that it is unfeminine for women to participate in political or public life and that they should only be concerned with domestic duties.

As women ... the first thing of importance is to be content to be inferior to men – inferior in mental power, in the same proportion that you are inferior in bodily strength.

Mrs Ellis, 1842

A good girl is tidy. A good girl makes herself pretty. A good girl is polite, docile, demure, submissive, passive, gentle, caring, giving, dependent, chaste. She stays out of trouble. Fighting is for boys, not girls. Learn these lessons well and you will get a gold star: a boyfriend, a ring, a husband, social approval.

from Jenny Beale, *Women in Ireland*, 1986

These views did not go unchallenged. Lots of women and some men fought back. They demanded equal rights, safeguarded by law. Mary Wollstonecraft was one of the first to challenge the view that women should be concerned only with domestic duties.

... what were we created for? To remain, it may be said, innocent; they mean in a state of childhood. We might as well never have been born, unless it were necessary that we should be created to enable man to acquire the noble privilege of reason, the power of discerning good from evil, whilst we lie down in the dust from whence we were taken, never to rise again.

Mary Wollstonecraft, *The Vindication of the Rights of Women*, 1792

William Thompson, the son of a wealthy Irish landowner, was even more radical in his beliefs. He claimed that men deliberately excluded women from participating in society:

To secure ... the advantages of superiority of strength, [man] makes the mind of his victim feeble ... by excluding from her, and serving to himself, all sources of knowledge and skill; by vesting in himself all power to create, all right to possess and control property; by excluding her from all those offices, actions, and incidents, which afford opportunities for exercising the judgment, and ... in the minutest incidents of life [making her] obedient to his will, be it wise or capricious.

William Thompson, *Appeal on Behalf of one Half of the Human Race, Women, Against the Pretensions of the other Half of the Human Race, Men, to Retain them in Political and thence in Civil and Domestic Slavery*, 1825

Those who demand the right of women to full and equal participation in society are referred to as 'feminists'. Feminism is the belief that men and women should be treated equally in all aspects of life.

STRUGGLE FOR THE RIGHT TO VOTE

The birth of modern feminism can be traced to the nineteenth century. Prior to this time, the majority of men and women worked within the home or on the land. The industrial revolution changed this. Women began to work outside the home in factories and mills, usually as cheap and casual labour. Side by side with this development, women from the upper and middle classes were entering universities and qualifying in medicine, teaching, and other professions.

Women began to exchange ideas and discuss political issues that affected them. They demanded equality of opportunity and the right to vote (suffrage). These women were known as 'suffragettes'.

The first women's rights meeting was convened in Seneca Falls, New York, in 1848. It declared that 'all men and women are created equal.' It demanded that women be given the vote.

At this time in Ireland, Catholic emancipation, land reform and Irish independence were the major issues. Many argued that women's equality should wait until these issues were resolved. Others disagreed.

The first Irish suffrage organisation was the Irish Women's Suffrage and Local Government Association (IWSLGA). It was founded in 1876 by Anna and Thomas Haslam, both Quakers, who have been described as 'Pioneers of Feminism in Ireland'. In 1908, the Irish Women's Franchise League (IWFL) was established by Hanna Sheehy-Skeffington and Margaret Cousins. Their more militant approach, holding public meetings and heckling politicians, was often controversial.

The Irish Women's Reform League was founded in 1911 by Louie Bennett to promote the interests of working women and to campaign for the right to vote. Later, as general secretary of the Irish Women Workers' Union (IWWU), she and others campaigned against child and domestic violence, for improvements in women's working conditions, for access to local government and the professions, and for birth control.

A limited right to vote for women was finally introduced in 1918. It was restricted to women over thirty years who owned property. Universal suffrage for all adults over the age of twenty-one was introduced in the constitution of the Irish Free State in 1922. These rights were confirmed in the 1937 constitution.

When the Right to Vote for Women was Won

New Zealand	1893	Netherlands	1919	Italy	1945
Australia	1902	Canada	1920	Japan	1945
Finland	1906	USA	1920	China	1949
Norway	1913	Ireland	1922	India	1949
Denmark	1915	Sri Lanka	1932	Mexico	1952
Soviet Union	1917	Brazil	1934	Egypt	1956
Britain	1918	Philippines	1937	Kenya	1964
Germany	1918	Jamaica	1944	Switzerland	1971
Poland	1918	France	1945	Jordan	1982

ASSIGNMENTS

1 Why did some people oppose the demand for women's equality?
2 What were considered the characteristics of an 'ideal' Irish woman? Is it the same today ?
3 Re-read the comments by Mary Wollstonecraft and William Thompson. How did they challenge the view that women should be content with domestic duties only?
4 Why were the women who demanded 'the vote' called 'suffragettes'?
5 Give a definition of feminism in your own words.
6 Women around the world have campaigned for decades for the right to vote. Why do you think it has taken so long to achieve?

RESEARCH ACTIVITIES

1 Look up information on one of the following suffragettes: Louie Bennett (Ireland), Helena Moloney (Ireland), Hanna Sheehy-Skeffington (Ireland), Emmeline Pankhurst (UK), Christabel Pankhurst (UK), Susan B. Anthony (USA), Elizabeth Cody Stanton (USA).
2 The Irish Women Workers' Union (IWWU) was the largest women's organisation in the country. In 1984 it merged with the Irish Transport and General Workers' Union, now SIPTU. Can you find out any information about it?

ACTIVITY

Organise a classroom discussion: Should Irish women have been prepared to postpone their campaign for suffrage until after political independence was won?

WOMEN IN IRISH SOCIETY

During the first half of this century, there were few opportunities for Irish women. If they lived in rural Ireland, they either married a farmer or left to be employed in domestic services. Life in the towns and cities was equally harsh, women often suffered from poverty and isolation. In the natural order of things men and women had different responsibilities. Most women married and had many children. Some became nuns or domestic servants, worked in laundries or emigrated.

The position of women in Irish society has changed dramatically since then. Side by side with economic growth and social development, new employment opportunities have become available.

The number of women working outside the home has risen sharply. Education has expanded to meet these new opportunities. More subject choice and career guidance is an integral part of the school curriculum.

The role of women in society has undergone considerable change in this century. At the beginning of the century, woman's place was generally regarded as being in the home. At that time, it was unthinkable to most men and many women that women should vote or (with rare exceptions) that they should engage in business or industry or join the professions. Nowadays women are progressively taking their rightful place in the community without detriment to family life. Increasing numbers of women join the professions – including such professions as accountancy, architecture, and engineering which were regarded until comparatively recently as the sole preserve of men. There are now women members of the judiciary and the Oireachtas, and of almost all local authorities; and women are to be found at all levels of business and industrial life.

Mr Justice Griffin in *De Búrca and Anderson v. Attorney General*, 1975

The modern Irish women's movement began in 1971. Public meetings, demonstrations, and a discussion on *The Late Late Show* sparked off a huge campaign which has affected everyone's life since then.

WHERE DID YOU WORK BEFORE YOU WORKED FOR US, MOM?

Today, Irish women are likely to make their own choices about their futures. Some opt to raise families and work in the home. Others choose to work outside the home in a wide range of jobs. Because more and more women continue to work after marriage, responsibilities in the home are likely to be shared.

These developments have affected family size. Traditionally, many women had four or more children. While most Irish women continue to see themselves as mothers and home-makers the number of children they have has fallen dramatically. Couples are choosing to limit their family size due to the cost of living, the uncertainty of secure employment, and choice of lifestyle. The use of natural and artificial contraceptives has risen sharply. Women and men are also choosing to marry later in life. All these factors have lowered the birth-rate.

What is a woman's most important role in life?

Motherhood/providing for family:	74%
Housewife/home-maker/wife:	27%
Shaping society:	7%
Self-fulfilment/being yourself:	6%
A career:	5%

The Irish Times/MRBI opinion poll of women's attitudes, 13 February, 1993

Attitudes towards women are changing in our society. Advertising which portrays women in a demeaning way is not allowed. Sexual harassment in the workplace is condemned. 'Girlie' photographs and calendars or sexually provocative remarks or actions are frowned upon. It is illegal for employers to pay women less money than their male colleagues for doing the same job. Discrimination against women in relation to employment, social welfare entitlements, jury service, education and taxation are also forbidden.

These changes have not benefited all women. Most women working outside the home are employed in low-paying, part-time work: cleaning, catering or unskilled factory work. The average hourly earning of Irish women is 68 per cent of men's. Many continue to live in

over-crowded housing conditions. Women are more at risk of poverty than men. Women in professional employment claim that a **'glass ceiling'** prevents them making their way to top jobs. Many women continue to suffer discrimination. Many are still subjected to sexual harassment in the workplace.

The idea that women should work outside the home is not universally supported. Some people believe that it is bad for young children if their mother goes out to work. There are not enough child-care facilities for women who wish or need to use them. In recent years, there has been a dramatic increase in reported cases of domestic violence, rape and incest.

glass ceiling:

refers to an invisible barrier preventing women's promotion to senior jobs beyond a certain point

Ms Michelle Ward on the assembly line at the Packard plant in Tallaght.

ASSIGNMENTS

1 How are attitudes towards women in Ireland changing? List some examples.
2 How would you define 'sexual harassment'? List some examples.
3 Why do you think 'girlie' photographs and calendars are prohibited in some workplaces? Do you agree or disagree with this?
4 Why have not all women benefited from the changes in attitudes towards women?
5 What do you think is a woman's most important role in life?
6 What do you think is a man's most important role in life?
7 Why do you think women rather than men are more likely to live in poverty today?

RESEARCH ACTIVITIES

1 Design a poster for an 'anti-sexual harassment' campaign.
2 Look at, and if possible record, some television advertisements that you feel are patronising towards women.
3 Read through some magazines and cut out the advertisements that you feel make women appear weak and submissive to men.

4   Select a workplace that you know or have access to (a business, a school, etc). List the various types of jobs there. Which tasks are done by men and which by women? Discuss the results in class.

5   Conduct a survey in your school or neighbourhood on 'What is a man's most important role in life?' Compare it with the survey on women's attitudes on page 194?

ACTIVITIES

1   Make a list of jobs that are typically chosen by women and another list of those typically chosen by men. Compare the different types of work.
   (a) Do the jobs for women require the same or different skills as those for men?
   (b) Do the jobs for women have the same social status as those for men?
   (c) Are the jobs for women likely to be paid more than, the same as, or less than, those for men?

2   Organise a classroom debate: That women should be paid for housework.

WOMEN AND THE LAW

Bunreacht na hÉireann (1937) guarantees political equality to all citizens – the right to vote and the right to stand for election. Some people, however, say that aspects of the constitution and of Irish law discriminates against women.

Article 41 presents a picture of family life as that of a married couple with children: the wife looks after children while the husband works outside the home to support the family. It refers to a woman's 'life within the home' and her 'duties in the home'. It warns against women being 'obliged ... to labour' outside the home.

This belief that men and women have specific roles in society has influenced Irish law. Equal rights for men and women at work are not guaranteed by the Irish constitution. The 'marriage bar', which prohibited married women from working,

was removed in 1973. Maternity leave has been available since 1981 but there is no paternity leave.

Eithne Fitzgerald was forced to resign in 1972 from the Department of Finance where she was employed as an economist when she married. Ironically, she became a junior minister in that Department, 1992–94.

If in 1970, you were in the civil service or semi-state employment, or working for the trade unions or the banks, you'd be expected to resign when you announced your marriage date. You might get rehired, but on their terms. In some places, it meant you would be on a temporary week-to-week hire basis as the company needed you. It would probably mean far less pay in a lower grade.

June Levine, *Sisters*, 1982

How does the criminal justice system treat women? Some people believe that the law does not adequately protect women who have been battered. Neither does it help women who have resorted to violence to defend themselves against their male partners.

… We were all waiting for the Ministers to come out in their state cars and we were going to shout at them … Mary [Anderson] and Mairín [de Búrca] were arrested … because the women opted for a trial by jury, and only then realised that a jury would consist of twelve property-owning men … Mairín asked Senator Mary Robinson how they could make a protest in court about being tried by twelve property-owning men without being sent down for contempt and she said: "you can't really make a protest in court without being sent down for contempt but what you could do is take a Constitutional action, because I believe that the Juries Act is, in fact, unconstitutional …

Regarding *De Búrca and Anderson vs the Attorney General* (1975) in June Levine, *Sisters*, 1982

Rape cases are another area of controversy. A woman is often accused of provoking her own rape because of the style of her clothing or because of 'flirtatious' behaviour.

Many people have asked the courts to rule on whether specific laws discriminate against women. It is now unconstitutional to deny women the right to sit on juries, but it is only unlawful to deny women equal pay at work or specific jobs. An equal rights amendment to the constitution is necessary to fully recognise equality of rights for women in all aspects of life.

Not long ago the legal profession was a male preserve. In 1990, for the first time, the number of women admitted as solicitors was more than the number of men. The number of women called to the bar has never exceeded the number of men. Among senior counsel, high-ranking barristers who earn the most money and from whom justices are chosen, women form a tiny minority. In 1995, there were 75 male and only 11 female judges in the country.

Mary Harney, leader of the Progressive Democrats.

197

ASSIGNMENTS

1 In what ways are women discriminated against?
2 What was the 'marriage bar'? How did it affect women?
3 Do you think men are discriminated against? List the ways.
4 Have you ever been discriminated against? Describe the incident.
5 Do you think women are better off today compared with twenty years ago?
6 Describe the ways in which the lives of rural and urban women in Ireland differ?
7 During periods of high unemployment, some people say that married women should be prevented from working. What do you think?
8 How do you think the criminal justice system treats women in cases of rape and domestic violence?

RESEARCH ACTIVITY

Talk to your grandmother, mother, aunt or neighbour about her life, her work in or outside the home, and her experiences as a woman growing up in Ireland. How does her life experience differ from your own?

ACTIVITIES

1 Organise a classroom discussion: What is the difference between something being unconstitutional and being unlawful? Why is an equal rights amendment to the constitution necessary to fully recognise equality of rights for women in all aspects of life?
2 Invite a representative from the trade union movement to talk to the class about equality of job opportunity, which jobs men and women do, and the importance of equality legislation.
3 Invite a representative from one of the following organisations to talk to the class about the lives of women in Ireland today: Irish Countrywoman's Association (ICA), Council for the Status of Women, AIM, the Rape Crisis Centre, the Women's Political Association, Women's Aid or the Travelling community.
4 Organise a classroom debate: That to reintroduce the 'marriage bar' for women would create more jobs and help reduce unemployment.
5 Organise a classroom debate: That a woman can provoke her own rape by the style of her clothing or 'flirtatious' behaviour.

WOMEN AND POLITICS

The whole point of a representative political system is to work within that system to bring about positive change and development. The consequences of our present imbalanced representation is that women's interests often have to be lobbied for from outside the Oireachtas and that issues of central concern to society, such as child care, community care, and flexibility in working life are compartmentalised as 'women's issues' and made marginal to the main political agenda of the day.

Second Commission on the
Status of Women, 1993

Politics is usually seen as a man's world. Only 10.5 per cent of the members of parliaments worldwide are women. Men set the political agenda, and shape and control the structures of state. Women claim that their absence from political life means that their interests and needs are ignored.

Women as a percentage of the members of national parliaments

Greece	5.3%
France	5.6%
U.K.	7.4%
Ireland	13%
Spain	14.6%
Germany	25.6%
Netherlands	30.2%
Denmark	33.0%

from *Women in Decision-Making*,
(2 ed) 1994, EU Commission

In common with international experience, women are under-represented in Irish political life and in the Oireachtas. With the exception of Constance Markievicz who was Minister for Labour in the government of the First Dáil in 1919, no woman held a cabinet post until Máire Geoghegan-Quinn became Minister for the Gaeltacht in December 1979.

To correct this inequality, the government in 1970 set up the Commission on the Status of Women. It produced a report on different aspects of women's lives. Its recommendations helped bring about equal pay and equality legislation, women's right to sit on juries, paid maternity leave, shelters for victims of domestic violence, and women's rights to the family home. Ireland's membership of the European Union has helped enforce these recommendations.

The Second Commission on the Status of Women published its report in 1993. It made 210 recommendations. Among these were

- an equal rights amendment to the Constitution to prohibit all forms of discrimination based on sex
- the appointment of a cabinet minister for women's affairs
- the removal of drink licences or other concessions from clubs and other facilities that discriminate against women.

The Women's Political Association (WPA) was founded in 1973 to help and encourage aspiring women politicians.

In 1978 two other organisations were set up: the Employment Equality Agency, a statutory body concerned with promoting and monitoring equality at work, and the Council for the Status of Women, a women's lobby group.

A junior minister for Women's Affairs and Family Law Reform was established in 1982. In 1983, the Joint Oireachtas Committee on Women's Rights was established. Greater priority was given to these issues with the establishment of a cabinet minister and a Department of Equality and Law Reform in 1993.

The election of Mary Robinson, the first president of the WPA, as president of Ireland in 1990 is an indication of the extent of change in people's attitudes and political interest in women's rights. The November 1992 general election returned twenty women TDs, the largest number ever. For the first time, two women were appointed to the cabinet.

All the political parties are now anxious to nominate women candidates and include 'women's issues' among their policies. Nevertheless, women remain absent from political life and decision-making generally. The number of candidates selected by political parties to contest elections is still low. Today, only about 10 per cent of candidates for the Dáil or Seanad are female.

Women are poorly represented in local government, on the judiciary, on the boards of semi-state companies, at the senior levels in the civil service, and on parliamentary committees. To help correct these inequalities, government appointments since 1993 must be made on the basis of 'gender-balance' – an equal number of men and women.

The growth in the number of women's interest groups has been very important. Many of these groups are now included in the consultation process before legislation is drawn up. Some have concentrated on putting together networks of professionals or experts who can be called upon for radio or television interviews, or for government committees. This form of activity has had varying degrees of success.

	Men		Women	
Membership of the 27th Dáil (elected November 1992)	145	(87%)	21	(13%)★
Membership of Seanad Éireann (elected January 1993)	52	(87%)	8	(13%)
Irish Members of European Parliament (elected June 1994)	11	(73%)	4	(27%)

★Kathleen Lynch (DL) was elected in a by-election in November 1994.

WHY SO FEW WOMEN IN PUBLIC LIFE?

crèche:

a nursery where children are cared for when their parents are at work, shopping, etc.

This chapter has shown that until recently, most women in Ireland have faced discrimination in law and public attitudes. Women's suffrage was actively discouraged. Women lived their lives primarily around their family and community. Few women became involved in public life or contested elections. Involvement in community or church affairs was the primary exception. Since 1970, much has changed.

We must look with fresh and unprejudiced eyes at the work of women, the views of women, their way of organising and their interpretation of social priorities. To achieve this, we must, I believe, begin at the beginning and alter our way of thinking.

President Mary Robinson, 1992

There is a growing interest among women to participate in political life. There is also greater public support for women candidates. In turn, women candidates are often seen by political strategists as a good means of maximising electoral support.

... in current analysis of what a party needs if it is to improve its vote, high profile women and possibly even a woman leader are at the top of most pundits' agenda ...

Úna Claffey, *The Women Who Won*, 1993

There is also increased acceptance in Ireland that women should have a greater and broader role in society. It is now quite common for women to work outside the home or become involved in community or public affairs. Yet, it can be very difficult to combine domestic responsibilities with other interests. This problem of the 'dual burden' does not affect men to the same extent. Once elected, the lack of adequate **crèche** facilities in the workplace, in the Oireachtas or in local authorities can act as an additional disincentive to women with young children.

... it is hard for women to get elected to Leinster House. The whole place is run to suit the male agenda. No matter what strides are made in terms of equality, at the end of the day the mother is still primarily responsible for the children, for their education, getting the meals on the table, making sure the school uniform is ready for Monday morning, making sure the homework is done, bringing the children to the doctor, sorting out all the problems that arise ... there isn't equality of opportunity.

Avril Doyle (Fine Gael TD) in Úna Claffey, *The Women Who Won*, 1993

Another obstacle to women's participation arises at the local level. Local government in Ireland is considered an essential stepping-stone to success in national politics. The low number of women on local councils makes it difficult for women to move up the next step in the political ladder. In addition, women do not have the range of contacts which might help them win elections. This might seem surprising because women make up the majority of members of parent/teacher's associations, church, and community and voluntary organisations.

Women have also been poorly represented on political party executives where most decisions are made about candidate selection. If women are not

201

selected in equal number to men to contest elections, then there will always be fewer women who win elections.

The cost of contesting elections can be very high. Political parties raise some of the money but individual candidates are expected to contribute to the election costs. Women who are not financially secure face additional burdens.

DOES UNDER-REPRESENTATION MATTER?

For most of the history of the Irish state, women have been under-represented in political and public affairs. Is it coincidental that over this same period Irish women have suffered discrimination in both legislation and public policy?

Since 1970, women's issues and questions of equality have received increased attention. Changes have been in line with developments and influences around the world. New legislation has been introduced. In turn, these developments have helped women participate more fully in public life and make choices about their lives.

Despite advances in women's rights, many serious problems remain:

- More child-care facilities are needed for women and men who wish to use them.
- The rise in reported domestic violence, rape and incest is very alarming.
- Many women and some men are subjected to sexual harassment in the workplace.
- The number of lone parents continues to rise.

Women TDs outside Leinster House.

- The continued presence of pornography and child pornography poses a threat to women and children.
- Many women remain trapped in low-skilled and poorly paid employment.
- Irish women are too often seen as dependants of their husbands rather than independent adults.

Many of the issues generally referred to as 'women's issues' are equally important for men. Like women, men have also found themselves restricted to a traditional lifestyle. Looking after children and nursing have usually been considered women's work. This is no longer the case.

It would be wrong to think that the solution to any or all of these problems will come about only with more women politicians. In some instances, male politicians have been to the forefront in pursuing change. These men are often referred to as feminist-males because of their support for feminist issues.

Yet, there is little doubt that the involvement of women in political life will have an important impact on legislation, public policy and women's status in society. After all, women are one half of the population!

ASSIGNMENTS

1 Despite advances in women's rights, many serious issues remain to be solved. Which of the following issues do you think are the most important? Which are the least important? Rank them in order with number 1 as the most important.
   (a) the provision of adequate child-care facilities for women and men who wish to use them
   (b) stiffer punishment for perpetrators of domestic violence, rape and incest
   (c) restrictions on, or abolition of, pornography and child pornography
   (d) an end to sexual harassment in the workplace
   (e) help for lone parents
   (f) widening educational and employment opportunities
   (g) the minimising of women's financial dependence on their husbands
   (h) an equal rights amendment to the constitution
   (i) other: _____.
2 Which other countries have a woman head of government or head of state? List these countries.
3 Does under-representation of women in politics matter? What do you think?
4 Name some obstacles to women's participation in politics.
5 How would you define the term 'women's issues'?
6 Which 'women's issues' do you think are equally important for men?

203

ACTIVITIES

1   Organise a classroom discussion on the most important issues that need to be solved to bring about equality between men and women in Irish society.

2   Invite a woman politician to your class to talk about the difficulties that she has experienced running for election.

3   Organise a classroom debate: That 'women's interests' can be represented equally well by a male as by a female politician.

4   Invite a representative from a local women's interest group to your classroom to talk about a campaign that they organised.

5   The following was published by the National Youth Council in the 1980's. Do you think any of the comments made still apply today?

Heard It Before??

HE

SHE

He works. She works. But my goodness, what different impressions they make.

You have of course encountered the double standard that operates at work. We still tend to use the old labels that say that women are emotional, disorganised and inefficient. Do you recognise the following situations?

HE	SHE
The family picture is on HIS desk. Ah, a solid, responsible family man.	**The family picture is on HER desk.** Umm, her family will come before her career.
His desk is cluttered. He's obviously a hard worker and a busy man.	**HER desk is cluttered.** She's obviously a disorganised scatterbrain.
He is talking with his co-workers. He must be discussing the latest deal.	**SHE is talking with her co-workers.** She must be gossiping.
HE'S not at his desk. He must be in a meeting.	**SHE'S not at her desk.** She must be in the ladies' room.
HE'S not in the office. He must be meeting customers.	**SHE'S not in the office.** She must be out shopping.
HE'S having lunch with the boss. He's on his way up.	**SHE'S having lunch with the boss.** They must be having an affair.
The boss criticized HIM. He'll improve his performance.	**The boss criticized HER.** She'll be very upset.
HE got an unfair deal. Did he get angry?	**SHE got an unfair deal.** Did she cry?
HE'S getting married. He'll get more settled.	**SHE'S getting married.** She'll get pregnant and leave.
HE'S having a baby. He'll need a raise.	**SHE'S having a baby.** She'll cost the company money in maternity benefits.
HE'S going on a business trip. It's good for his career.	**SHE'S going on a business trip.** What does her husband say?
HE'S leaving for a better job. He knows how to recognise a good opportunity.	**SHE'S leaving for a better job.** Women are not dependable.

Courtesy of the National Youth Council of Ireland

CHAPTER 11

NORTHERN IRELAND

A PLACE APART

*T*hey *[the British and Irish Governments]
acknowledge that in Northern Ireland,
unlike the situation which prevails
elsewhere throughout both islands, there is a
fundamental absence of consensus about
constitutional issues. There are deep divisions
between the members of the two main traditions
living there over their respective senses of identity
and allegiance, their views on the present status of
Northern Ireland and their vision of future
relationships in Ireland and between the two
islands …*

A New Framework for Agreement, 1995

Conflicts over territory and national
identity are common throughout history.

Cyprus is divided because Greek Cypriots
and Turkish Cypriots can not agree.
Serbia and Croatia have fought a bloody
war over territory, while Palestine has
been the centre of a bitter conflict since
the UN gave the land, now known as
Israel, to the Jews after WWII.

The conflict in Northern Ireland is also
about territory and identity. It involves two
communities, each of which claims a
different political allegiance. Nationalists are
usually members of the Catholic faith; they
favour a united Ireland. Unionists come
from various Protestant denominations and
favour Northern Ireland remaining in the
United Kingdom.

I would be anti-British, in the sense that ... when I look at history and see people starving and these boys sitting with their sacks of corn and I see the amount of money that they've taken out of Ireland, landlordism, the Catholics living up in the bare Sperrins and down around Lough Neagh's shores ... you begin to think – that's what they've done to us.

from Fionnuala O'Connor, *In Search of a State. Catholics in Northern Ireland*, 1993

They the Protestants loved the old flag, the emblem of liberty and justice, they wanted to remain exactly as they were, loyal subjects to the King of the British Empire ... if the government tried to force, to compel them to submit to the domination of a parliament in Dublin largely composed of agriculturalists, who knew absolutely nothing of their requirements, then that force would be met by a resistance stronger than the most optimistic could image.

George Stevens, *Belfast News Letter*, 29 April 1914

non-sectarian:

non-sectarian is not narrowly limiting membership of a society to members of a single religious, ethnic or racial group

Stories and pictures of the Troubles in Northern Ireland have dominated our newspapers, radios and televisions over the past twenty five years. Despite widespread news coverage, myth, prejudice and misunderstanding have strongly influenced our (mis)understanding of the conflict.

The two communities have different fears and aspirations. Many see the other's traditions and views as alien, threatening, and foreign. Few people have the opportunity to socialise with people from the opposite tradition. Consequently, each views the other with suspicion. The chart below lists some reasons for this mistrust.

There are also many people in Northern Ireland who do not identify with, or wish to be identified with, either 'nationalism' or 'unionism'. They want to see a **non-sectarian** Northern Ireland.

Today, politicians have the very difficult task of reconciling these opposing points of view.

UNIONISTS	NATIONALISTS
• want to live in the United Kingdom and be British citizens	• want to live in a united Ireland and be Irish citizens
• want to protect their traditions	• want 'parity of esteem' – to have their religious beliefs and cultural traditions recognised and valued
• want to preserve their political power as the majority in Northern Ireland	• want their rights as the minority within Northern Ireland protected
• fear losing their religious freedom and political status in a united Ireland.	• believe unionists are incapable of sharing power in any future Northern Ireland.

HISTORICAL BACKGROUND

*B*oth Governments recognise that there is much for deep regret on all sides in the long and often tragic history of Anglo-Irish relations, and of relations in Ireland ...
A New Framework for Agreement, 1995

The Anglo-Normans invaded Ireland in 1169 and began to establish basic political structures. Their conquest of the entire island did not, however, begin until the Tudor dynasty of the 16th century.

By 1603, the last of the Gaelic 'chiefs' had been defeated. In their place, James I began to settle subjects he could trust. The 'plantation of Ulster' in 1607 replaced Catholics with 170,000 Protestant settlers throughout central Ulster.

Later, under Oliver Cromwell, Commander-in-Chief and Lord Lieutenant of Ireland (1649-1650) and his son Henry, thousands of acres of Irish land were given to English investors ('adventurers') and soldiers. Approximately 2,000 Catholic families were resettled on smaller holdings in the west. The victory of settlers over native Irish was confirmed when Protestant William of Orange defeated Catholic James II in the Battle of the Boyne in 1690.

These events established Protestant settlers or 'planters' as the landowning and 'ruling class' throughout Ireland. In contrast, Catholics suffered from the political, legal, economic and psychological effects of defeat. The Penal Laws, 1695 and 1704, restricted their rights to education, to bear arms, to own a horse worth more than five pounds, and to own businesses. In 1728, the right to vote was formally removed.

... it is necessary for understanding my history to take a rapid survey of the state of parties in Ireland ...

... the Protestants, though not above the tenth of the population, were in possession of the whole of the government, of five-sixths of the landed property of the nation; they were, and had been, for above a century, in the quiet enjoyment of the church, the laws, the revenue, the army, the navy, the magistracy, the corporations; in a word, of the whole patronage of Ireland ...

The Catholics ... were above two-thirds of the nation, and formed, perhaps, a still greater proportion. They embraced the entire peasantry of three provinces, they constituted a considerable portion of the mercantile interest, but, from the tyranny of the penal laws ... they possessed but a very small proportion of the landed property ... Suffice it to say, that there was no injustice, no disgrace, no disqualification, moral, political, or religious, civil or military, that was not heaped upon them ...
Theobald Wolfe Tone, *Autobiography*, 1893

Irish nationalism was influenced by the French Revolution, 1789. **Theobald Wolfe Tone** (1763-98) helped form the Society of United Irishmen in 1791. Its aim was to unite 'Catholic, Protestant and Dissenter' and to win parliamentary

Theobald Wolfe Tone
Tone is known as the 'Father of Irish Republicanism' because of the United Irishman's aim of an Irish republic.

reform. The failure to win agreements from an exclusively Protestant Irish parliament, known as Grattan's Parliament (1782-1800), forced the United Irishmen to consider revolution. The rising of 1798 was forcibly put down. Robert Emmet's rising of 1803 met a similar fate. To prevent a reoccurrence, Ireland was joined to the United Kingdom of England, Scotland and Wales under the Act of Union in 1800.

Throughout the 19th century, the two communities grew further apart, each with their own political allegiance. Already, there were differences of religious belief, language, culture and customs, and degree of technical development. A pattern of 'uneven economic development' added to these differences.

In Ulster, economic prosperity after 1780 led to a rapid expansion in linen and cotton manufacturing, brewing, and later shipbuilding and engineering. This growth was confined primarily to the Lagan Valley around Belfast. Strong trade links developed with northern England and Scotland. As a consequence, both Protestant industrialists and skilled workers saw the Act of Union as beneficial. They desired further integration with the British economy. This was particularly important for workers who earned much more than their counterparts in Dublin. By the 1880s, defence of the Union had become linked to defence of Protestantism.

Southern Ireland's manufacturing suffered under the Union. Its economy remained dependent on agriculture but the land had been over-subdivided. Irish tenants survived by growing potatoes on small plots of land. The Great Famine (1845-1851) was the result of a series of crop failures. Over 1 million people died of starvation and 1.5 million emigrated. Political campaigns for Catholic Emancipation (achieved 1829) and Repeal of the Union, led by Daniel O'Connell and the Young Irelanders, linked Catholic rights with the demand for Irish independence.

Tension between the opposing interests and demands of nationalists and unionists reached a peak at the end of the 19th century. Demands by one side led to counter-demands or actions by the other. The Fenian Rising occurred in 1867. The threat of home rule or limited independence encouraged many Protestants to join the Orange Order. Unionists successfully prevented the passage of three home rule bills (1886, 1893, 1912). While Britain was distracted by the First World War, Irish nationalists participated in the Easter Rising, 1916. This was followed by the equally bloody Anglo-Irish War or War of Independence, 1919-1921.

Failure to agree on the future of Ireland led to its partitioning. The Government of Ireland Act, 1920, formally divided the island. In 1921, a self-governing Irish state was established in the southern 26 counties, while the northern 6 counties stayed in the United Kingdom.

ASSIGNMENTS

1   Look again at the different aspirations of nationalism and unionism listed on page 207. Why do you think each community sees the other's traditions and views as alien, threatening, and foreign?

2   What developments led to the origins of Ulster unionism?

3   What were the origins of Irish nationalism?

4   Why are nationalists also referred to as republicans?

5   Why do unionists have a strong association with the colour orange?

6   Orangemen and women march on the 12th of July to celebrate the Battle of the Boyne. Why do the Apprentice Boys march in Derry on the 12th of August each year?

7   Nationalists call the city 'Derry'. What do unionists call it? Why?

RESEARCH ACTIVITIES

1   Explain the historical significance of one of the following events:
    (a) the Norman conquest of Ireland in 1169
    (b) the plantation of Ulster in 1610
    (c) the defeat of King James II by William of Orange in 1690
    (d) the United Irishmen Rising of 1798
    (e) the Act of Union of 1800
    (f) the Home Rule Bills of 1886, 1893, 1912

2   Irish nationalists remember the events of the 1916 Rising as an important landmark in the struggle for Irish independence. In the same year, thousands of Ulster Protestants fought and died as members of the British Army at the Battle of the Somme July 1916 during WWI.
    (a) Can you find out any information about this event?
    (b) Do these two events represent different Irish traditions and allegiances?
    (c) Huge numbers of Catholics, north and south, also enlisted during the Great War. Can you find out any information about them?

ACTIVITY

Read or go see Frank McGuinness' play: 'Observe the Sons of Ulster Marching Towards the Somme'.

(a) How does the play give us an insight into the lives of Ulstermen?

(b) What view of WWI is portrayed in the play?

(c) Why do you think that this event holds great significance for the Protestant community in Ireland?

THE NORTHERN IRELAND STATE

Faced with the rise of Sinn Féin after the 1918 general election, British political elites were divided over how to react. However, all agreed that Ulster Unionists could not be coerced into a united Ireland. In the end, partition was the only solution to an intractable problem. The Northern Ireland state was born in 1921 and formalised in 1925 when the Boundary Commission agreed to leave the border as it was.

From the beginning, many unionists worried about Britain's long-term intentions: did Britain wish to withdraw? Others felt nationalist desires for Irish unity were disloyal. Over the next decades, decisions by the Irish government to include aspects of Catholic social and moral teaching in legislation and the constitution raised further fears. Stories were told of Protestants forced to flee from the south. Unionists felt

B-Specials:

B-Specials were the part-time, but fully armed, section of the Ulster Special Constabulary established in 1920. It was an entirely Protestant force.

justified in creating a state giving Protestants preferential treatment.

There are only two classes in Northern Ireland: the loyal and the disloyal. The loyal people are the Orangemen. The disloyal are the Socialists, Communists and Roman Catholics.
Unionist Backbencher quoted in Paul Arthur, *Government and Politics of Northern Ireland*, 1980

From the foundation of the Northern Ireland state, many nationalists withheld their support. They saw the state as sectarian (anti-Catholic) and discriminatory. They believed many of the laws and political institutions were designed to maintain the privilege of the unionist population. They maintained that:

- the **B-Specials** were a sectarian Protestant force
- the Special Powers Act was a draconian piece of legislation which denied civil rights
- the practice of 'gerrymandering', drawing local government constituency boundaries to suit the governing party, insured a unionist majority even when there wasn't one
- voting by proportional representation, abolished for local elections in 1922 and for Northern Ireland parliamentary elections in 1929, ensured a unionist majority
- the Representation of the People Bill, 1946, restricted the right to vote by taking it away from lodgers
- employment and housing allocation was determined on religious criteria.

211

Catholics in Northern Ireland were primarily represented by the Nationalist Party which periodically refused to attend the parliament because of its domination by the Unionist Party.

It is undeniable that the government of Northern Ireland are to be blamed for the manner in which they conducted the affairs of their state in the half century which followed the Anglo-Irish Treaty of 1921, and that they must bear much of the responsibility for the outbreak of the troubles of our own time. But it is unhistorical and unfair to allot such blame and responsibility without also reiterating why the Northern Ireland government came to behave as they did ...

Robert Kee, *Ireland. A History*, 1980

NORTHERN IRELAND POLITICAL SYSTEM

A Protestant parliament for a Protestant people.

James Craig, Prime Minister of Northern Ireland, 1934

A Northern Ireland parliamentary system based on Westminster was established in 1921. It had a bicameral parliament with an upper house or Senate with 26 members, and a lower house or House of Commons with 52 members. Elections for five years were initially by single transferable vote (STV) although this was changed to a simple majority in 1929.

In 1932, a parliament building at Stormont, a Belfast suburb, was completed. The word 'Stormont' has often been used to refer to the unionist-controlled government.

The British monarch was represented by the Governor who was appointed for six years. The Governor appointed ministers to the Northern Ireland cabinet, dissolved parliament, delivered the Queen's speech at the start of each parliamentary session, and could withhold consent for legislation.

The powers of the Northern Ireland parliament were limited to matters concerning its own territory and it could not legislate on the armed forces, foreign affairs, external trade, coinage, etc. In theory, it was subservient to the British Parliament. In practice, however, from 1923-1960, the British government and parliament were happy to let the Unionists run Northern Ireland without serious attempts to interfere. Since 1972, Northern Ireland has been ruled directly from London.

ASSIGNMENTS
1 Why was partition considered the only solution? Do you think another solution was possible?
2 Why did unionists feel apprehensive and worried about Britain's intentions?
3 Why did unionists view the Republic as a foreign and hostile state?
4 How do you think the privilege of the unionist population was maintained?
5 What is Stormont?

THE TROUBLES

In 1963, Terence O'Neill (1963-69) was elected prime minister of Northern Ireland. Faced with serious economic problems, he set about modernising the economy and proposing political reforms. He also sought better relations with the Republic, beginning with a meeting between himself and Taoisigh Seán Lemass in 1965 and Jack Lynch in 1967.

O'Neill's actions were strongly criticised by many unionists who did not wish to see any change in Protestant privilege. In contrast, they encouraged Catholics who were looking for change. Ultimately, the failure to introduce reforms quickly enough led to the formation of the Northern Ireland Civil Rights Association (NICRA).

Ulster stands at the crossroad ... For more than five years now I have tried to heal some of the deep divisions in our community. I did so because I could not see how an Ulster divided against itself could hope to stand. I made it clear that a Northern Ireland based upon the interests of any one section rather than upon the interests of all could have no long-term future ...

Terence O'Neill, December 9, 1968

NICRA was formed in 1967 to challenge the sectarian and discriminatory aspects of the Stormont regime. It called for:

- a universal franchise, 'one man, one vote' in local government elections
- redrawing of electoral boundaries to end gerrymandering
- the introduction of laws to end discrimination in local government employment
- a compulsory points system for public housing to ensure every applicant is treated equally
- the repeal of the Special Powers Act
- the disbandment of the B-specials.

A confrontation between civil rights campaigners and the police in Derry city on 5 October, 1968 marked the beginning of the modern Ulster crisis or 'Troubles'. The events were broadcast by television around the world.

We came to Burntollet Bridge [near Derry], and from lanes at each side of the road a curtain of bricks and boulders and bottles brought the march to a halt. From the lanes burst hordes of screaming people wielding planks of wood, bottles, laths, iron bars, crowbars, cudgels studded with nails, and they waded into the march beating hell out of everybody ...

Bernadette Devlin, *The Price of My Soul*, 1969

Seán Lemass and Terence O'Neill, 1965.

213

Several events intensified the conflict from the start:

- A march between Belfast City Hall and Derry was attacked on 4 January, 1969 by about 200 Unionists, including off-duty members of the B-specials. The 'Battle for the Bogside' [Derry] was the name given to a riot sparked off when a parade by the Apprentice Boys passed by the Catholic Bogside on 12 August, 1969. The rioting quickly spread to other parts of Northern Ireland. 'No-go' areas, where government security forces were prevented from operating, were set up. The first victims, a nine year old Catholic boy and two Protestant men, were killed on 14 August, 1969.
- By August 1969, the British cabinet decided to send in the Army to keep order and protect the Catholic community from sectarian attack. The 'breakdown in public order' continued, and internment or detention without trial was introduced on 9 August 1971. On 30 January 1972, the Parachute Regiment shot dead thirteen men, all unarmed, at the end of a civil rights rally in Derry. The event became known as 'Bloody Sunday'.
- Sections of the Catholic and Protestant communities became increasingly more hostile towards each other. The Provisional IRA launched a paramilitary campaign to force the British to withdraw from Northern Ireland and to bring about a united Ireland. Protestant extremists formed the Ulster Defence Force (UDA) and revitalised the Ulster Volunteer Force (UVF). As a result of continued political instability, Stormont was abolished and 'direct rule' from London was introduced in February 1972. The Northern Ireland Parliament met for the last time on 28 March.

British soldiers on duty in Northern Ireland.

Over the years, the campaign for civil rights was transformed into a sectarian conflict. Catholics became increasingly hostile towards the state while Protestants feared that Northern Ireland was under threat. Sectarian, violent and murderous confrontations between Catholics and Protestants became commonplace. Rioting and burning of homes forced thousands of families to flee their homes; approximately ten per cent of Belfast's population had moved by February 1973. Catholics moved out of east and north Belfast, and Protestants moved out of west Belfast.

People in the Republic looked on in disbelief and horror as the events in Northern Ireland unfolded.

It is clear now that the present situation cannot be allowed to continue. It is evident that the Stormont government cannot be allowed to continue. It is evident that the Stormont government is no longer in control of the situation. Indeed the present situation is the inevitable outcome of the policies pursued for decades by successive Stormont governments. It is clear also that the Irish government can no longer stand by and see innocent people injured and perhaps worse.

Taoiseach Jack Lynch, 13 August, 1969

'Bloody Sunday' provoked a demonstration in Dublin, and the burning of the British Embassy, then on Merrion Square. In May 1970, two former Fianna Fail ministers, Charles Haughey and Neil Blaney, appeared in court accused of plotting to smuggle arms to the IRA. Both were acquitted. In their defence, they claimed that the weapons were part of an officially sanctioned Irish Army operation. It was later alleged that their action helped form the Provisional IRA.

ASSIGNMENTS

1 Why was the Northern Ireland Civil Rights Association formed?
2 What reforms did Terence O'Neill introduce? Why did unionists oppose these reforms?
3 What events contributed to transforming the civil rights campaign into a sectarian conflict?
4 What was the reaction of people in the Irish Republic to events in Northern Ireland?

RESEARCH ACTIVITIES

1 Write an essay on the role played by one of the following people in the events in Northern Ireland: Edward Carson, James Craig, Terence O'Neill, John Hume, Gerry Adams, John Alderdice, James Molyneux, Ian Paisley and Gerry Fitt.
2 Write to one of the major political parties in Northern Ireland asking them for their view on current political developments and their proposals for resolving the conflict.

MAIN POLITICAL PARTIES

Official Unionist Party (OUP) ruled Northern Ireland since the formation of the state in 1921 until Direct Rule was introduced in March 1972. It was formed in 1905 as the Ulster Unionist Party (UUP) to resist demands for Home Rule. It is the largest political party in Northern Ireland and of Protestants, and is strongest in rural areas and among the middle class. On social and economic issues, the OUP is conservative. It favours some form of Northern Ireland assembly or 'devolution', the establishment of Northern Ireland political structures while remaining within the United Kingdom. It is opposed to the formation of any all-Ireland institutions which might give the Irish government any role in the running of Northern Ireland.

Democratic Unionist Party (DUP) was founded in 1971 by the Rev. Ian Paisley. It has successfully mixed sectarianism and radical policies. It strongly favours keeping the constitutional link between Northern Ireland and the UK, and opposes any co-operation with the Republic. After the Anglo-Irish Agreement, it accused the British of 'selling out Ulster'. The DUP supports some form of devolution. On social and economic issues, it is broadly left-of-centre. It opposes public expenditure cuts. Its hard line on security has a strong appeal in Protestant working class areas which have been most affected by the Troubles.

Social Democratic and Labour Party (SDLP) was founded in August 1970. It succeeded the Nationalist Party which had been the major Catholic political organisation with representatives at Stormont. Over the years, it has become more nationalist, concerned with representing the interests of Catholics and seeking an 'agreed Ireland' solution. It favours strong links with Dublin and the European Union even if this means 'going over the heads of Unionists'. In 1992, John Hume (its leader) began extensive talks with Gerry Adams (President of Sinn Féin) which led ultimately to the ceasefire in 1994. It is broadly left-of-centre on social and economic issues, and has its greatest support among the growing Catholic middle class.

The Alliance Party was founded in 1970 by Unionists, liberals and members of the New Ulster Movement who supported reforms. It favours building an 'alliance' between Catholics and Protestants to promote moderate and anti-sectarian policies. Its greatest support is among the middle class. It favours devolving more authority to Northern Ireland.

Sinn Féin (Provisional) is the political wing of the Provisional Irish Republican Army (IRA). It was formed in 1969. It pursued an 'armed struggle' (bombings and killings of members of the security forces and Protestant civilians) to force the British to withdraw from Northern Ireland, weaken Unionist resistance, and unite the 'six counties' of Ulster with the Republic. These bombing campaigns were also targeted at financial and political institutions and personalities in Britain. At the same time, Sinn Féin conducted a political campaign aimed at winning international endorsement, and electoral support in Northern Ireland. This two-handed approach was called 'with a ballot box in one hand and an armalite in the other'. It is strong among unemployed urban Catholic communities in Northern Ireland but it has little support in the Republic except in border counties. On 31 August 1994, the IRA announced 'a complete cessation of military activities'.

STEPS TO PEACE

Since 1973, British and Irish politicians, civil servants and church leaders have been involved in open and secret talks with political and paramilitary leaders in Northern Ireland. Several political proposals have been discussed and/or implemented.

These plans have called for a new administration which would be supported by the entire community. They include the idea of 'power-sharing' – dividing power between the Catholic-nationalist and Protestant-unionist communities. They support the need for consultation and co-operation between Northern Ireland and the Republic, often referred to as the 'Irish Dimension'.

The Northern Ireland Assembly was established after elections on 28 June 1973. A 'power-sharing' executive with representatives from the Ulster Unionists, Alliance and SDLP took office on 1 January 1974. Brian Faulkner (Unionist) became the Chief Executive, and Gerry Fitt (SDLP) the Deputy Chief Executive. William Craig (Vanguard Unionist Party) and Ian Paisley (Democratic Unionist Party) opposed it. Five months later, a large work stoppage affecting factories and power stations throughout Northern Ireland was organised by the (Unionist) Ulster Workers Council in protest against the executive. The executive collapsed.

The Sunningdale Agreement was the result of the first conference since 1925 between government representatives of Britain and both parts of Ireland (6 December 1973). Britain was represented by the Prime Minister Ted Heath and the Republic by Taoiseach Liam Cosgrave. The main aim was to give effect to the 'Irish Dimension'. It decided to establish a Council of Ireland with representatives from Northern Ireland and the Republic, and a Consultative Assembly.

From the start, people had different views of the Council of Ireland's purpose. Brian Faulkner (Unionist) believed it would be concerned only with cross-border issues, such as tourism, transport and agriculture. The SDLP, however, believed it would lead to all-Ireland institutions and eventually to an agreed single (united) Ireland.

Sunningdale collapsed when the power-sharing executive fell.

New Ireland Forum was established by the Irish government in March 1983 and met for the first time on 30 May. It brought together the SDLP, FF, FG and Labour to develop a joint approach to the Northern Ireland situation.

After hearing and receiving hundreds of submissions from political, religious and community organisations, and individuals, it concluded that a unitary state would resolve the problems.

The Anglo-Irish Agreement was signed between Taoiseach Garret FitzGerald and Prime Minister Margaret Thatcher on 15 November 1985 at Hillsborough Castle, Co. Down. It was a binding international agreement, the first since 6 December, 1921.

Article 1(a) stated that the two governments 'affirm that any change in the status of Northern Ireland would only come about with the consent of the majority of the people of Northern Ireland'.

The Agreement proposed the establishment of an Inter-Governmental Conference to meet regularly and deal with political, security and legal matters, and the promotion of cross-border co-operation. It also introduced measures to recognise 'the two traditions in Northern Ireland, to protect human rights and to prevent discrimination'. Britain agreed it would support a united Ireland if the majority of the population in Northern Ireland consented.

The Agreement gave the Republic its greatest involvement in Northern Ireland affairs although it was not the 'joint authority' that some nationalists wanted. Unionists, however, were very angry. They believed it was further evidence of British betrayal – that the British were anxious to withdraw completely from Northern Ireland.

There was also criticism in the Republic. Mary Robinson, then a Senator, resigned from the Labour Party because the Agreement was 'unacceptable to all sections of unionist opinion.'

A permanent secretariat of civil servants from both the Republic and Britain was established at Maryfield, County Down. In addition, a joint parliamentary committee was formed.

Joint Declaration for Peace and Reconciliation (Downing Street Declaration) was signed on 15 December 1993 between Taoiseach Albert Reynolds and Prime Minister John Major.

The Declaration acknowledged the conflicting demands of the two communities: the desire by unionists to remain within the United Kingdom, and that of nationalists for a united Ireland. It reaffirmed that any change in the status of Northern Ireland could only come about through the consent of the people of Northern Ireland 'freely given'. Britain would accept any decision made by people in Northern Ireland even for a united Ireland. It claimed it had no 'selfish strategic or economic interest' in remaining in Northern Ireland.

By formally recognising the aspirations of nationalists, the Declaration hoped to persuade the IRA to give-up violence. The USA also pledged to help resolve the conflict. On 31 August 1994, the IRA declared a ceasefire. A loyalist paramilitary ceasefire was declared on 13 October 1994.

The Forum for Peace and Reconciliation began meeting in Dublin Castle in December 1994. It provides an opportunity for political parties and others to exchange views. No unionist party has participated in these discussions because they believe it is laying the ground for a united Ireland.

A New Framework for Agreement, signed by Taoiseach John Bruton and Prime Minister John Major on 22 February 1995, outlined a joint British-Irish proposal for the future of Northern Ireland. The proposals suggest:
- the establishment of a cross-border body with 'executive' and 'harmonising' powers in a wide range of areas, including tourism, health and education

- balanced constitutional changes to Articles 2 and 3 of the Irish constitution, and the Government of Ireland Act, 1920.

The national territory consists of the whole island of Ireland, its islands and the territorial seas.

Pending the re-integration of the national territory, and without prejudice to the right of the Parliament and Government established by this Constitution to exercise jurisdiction over the whole of that territory, the laws enacted by that Parliament shall have the like area and extent of application as the laws of Saorstat Éireann and the like extra-territorial effect.

Articles 2 and 3, *Bunreacht na hÉireann*

At the same time, the British government published its plans for a new Northern Ireland assembly.

… the British Government recognise that it is for the people of Ireland alone, by agreement between the two parts respectively and without external impediment, to exercise their right of self-determination on the basis of consent, freely and concurrently given, North and South, to bring about a united Ireland, if that is their wish; the Irish Government accept that the democratic right of self-determination by the people of Ireland as a whole must be achieved and exercised with and subject to the agreement and consent of a majority of the people of Northern Ireland.

A New Framework for Agreement, 1995

Public and political opinion of both the Joint Declaration and the Framework Document has been mixed. Nationalists have been happy because they believe it holds out the promise of a united Ireland. Unionists have been unhappy. They believe it paves the way for a united Ireland despite reassurances that the status of Northern Ireland can not be changed without a referendum of the people in Northern Ireland.

ASSIGNMENTS

1. Explain the following terms in your own words:
   (a) Irish Dimension
   (b) joint authority
   (c) consent 'freely given'
2. How did the Joint Declaration attempt to reconcile the conflicting demands of the two communities in Northern Ireland?
3. Why were unionists **unhappy** with the Joint Declaration and the Framework documents? Why were nationalists **happy** with them?

ACTIVITY

Organise a classroom discussion: The Irish government has pledged that it will amend the constitution to remove the 'territorial claim' of the Republic over Northern Ireland found in Articles 2 and 3. Do you agree with this?

NORTHERN IRELAND TODAY

While no one can predict a solution to the conflict in Northern Ireland with any confidence, there have been enormous changes since the beginning of the Troubles in 1968. The key demands of the Northern Ireland Civil Rights Association have been met long ago. Direct rule from London has taken decision-making away from the unionist-controlled parliament at Stormont, and from local councils.

Other changes include:

- a universal franchise, 'one man, one vote' introduced, 1969, for all elections
- an independent electoral boundary commission determines constituency boundaries
- the Fair Employment Act, 1976, made it illegal to discriminate in employment on religious or political grounds, and established the Fair Employment Agency
- the Northern Ireland Housing Executive, established by law in 1971, was given responsibility for public authority house-building and allocation
- the Special Powers Act was abolished in 1973 and replaced by the Emergency Provisions Act
- the B-specials were replaced by the Ulster Defence Regiment (UDR) in 1970
- the Republic of Ireland government has an influential voice in Northern Ireland affairs.

Life for many has also changed in Northern Ireland. While northern nationalists once felt themselves to be living in an 'alien' state, many are now part of the political and economic mainstream.

The Catholic middle class is now the fastest growing force in Northern Irish society. In contrast, young Protestants tend to emigrate as university students and never return. This will have the effect of reducing the size of the Protestant middle class.

In 1973, only 5 per cent of Northern Ireland civil servants were Catholics although they represented 33 per cent of the population. By 1992, Catholics were over-represented in the civil service. The greatest level of change can be seen in the students at Queens University, Belfast. Before 1970, 70 per cent were Protestant; by 1993, Catholics equalled more than 50 per cent.

The speed with which Catholic lawyers, doctors, accountants, and entrepreneurs of various kinds have developed access to political decision-making, and made their way into an economic mainstream once largely closed to them, has left nerves jangling inside the Catholic community and beyond it. In such a small society, and because the public face of Northern Ireland was formerly Protestant to such a degree, economically successful Catholics ... make an impression disproportionate to their numbers. Clustered in the comfortable suburbs, particularly in Derry, Dungannon, Newry and Belfast, the newly arrived have in addition developed a reputation as free-spending, confident and optimistic, an image that increases their impact.

Fionnuala O'Connor, *In Search of a State. Catholics in Northern Ireland*, 1993